# PITTSBURGH—
## METROPOLITAN MASTERY

# PITTSBURGH—
## METROPOLITAN MASTERY

### TRAVEL GUIDE (AND MORE)
### OF THE STEEL CITY

## Rock DiLisio

# PITTSBURGH— METROPOLITAN MASTERY
## TRAVEL GUIDE (AND MORE) OF THE STEEL CITY

iUniverse books may be ordered through booksellers or by contacting:

iUniverse
1663 Liberty Drive
Bloomington, IN 47403
www.iuniverse.com
1-800-Authors (1-800-288-4677)

ISBN: 978-1-5320-3364-3 (sc)
ISBN: 978-1-5320-3365-0 (e)

Print information available on the last page.

iUniverse rev. date:  10/02/2017

# Contents

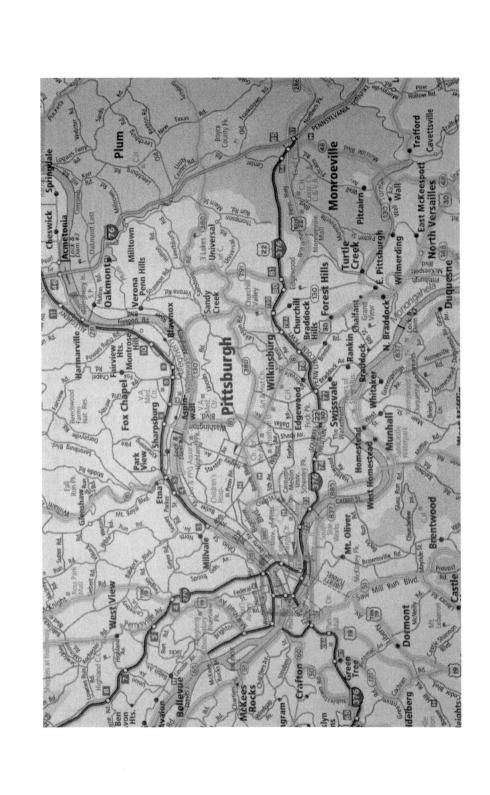

Nestled in the foothills of the Appalachian Mountains and guarding three powerful rivers, Pittsburgh is the sentinel of America. The French and Indian War (the first true world war) was primarily fought over who would control this strategic location. Once the British wrestled the sacred ground from the French, Pittsburgh became the eternal *Gateway to the West*.

As a portal to American westward expansion, Pittsburgh provided the natural resources and industrial goods to build this great country. The Steel City has been a refined combination of strength and beauty – a combination not often found in a metropolis. A city that projects one of the world's most impressive skylines, incorporating gleaming buildings of steel and glass situated within hills, valleys and lush foliage. Without leaving the county proper, Pittsburgh surprisingly moves from metropolis to farmland within a short drive. Yes, this is the American city often compared to the beauty of Paris, France and St. Petersburg, Russia and in the same instance, still often named as *America's Most Livable City*.

*As long as the Monongahela and Allegheny shall flow to form the Ohio; as long as the English tongue shall be the language of freedom in the boundless valleys which these waters traverse, Pittsburgh shall stand as the Gateway of the West.*

# Chapter 1

# ACCOLADES FOR THE CITY

*Compliments are often the best realization of identity. Some of the world's most renowned publications and citizens have commented on the city called...Pittsburgh:*

- *The three most beautiful cities in the world are Paris; St. Petersburg, Russia; and Pittsburgh. If Pittsburgh were situated somewhere in the heart of Europe, tourists would eagerly journey hundreds of miles out of their way to visit it. Its setting is spectacular . . .*

  **Brendan Gill - *The New Yorker*, January 1989**

- *Steeped in spirit and flavor, Pittsburgh can lay claim to being one of our nation's most underrated cities, with a beauty as breathtaking as it is obvious. The drive from Pittsburgh International Airport follows an unspectacular 20 miles of rolling-hills suburbia along Interstate Highway 376 and then, after a brief trip through the Fort Pitt Tunnel — bam! — there is Pittsburgh.*

  *Situated on a peninsula jutting into an intersection of rivers, the city of 305,000 is gemlike, surrounded by bluffs and bright yellow bridges streaming into its heart. As you emerge from the tunnel, you feel you've never seen a more majestic little city: old but familiar, with swooping, curving lines, lushly green (in summer) and cut, as all great cities should be, by a river or two (or in this case, three).*

1

*Visiting is the only way to understand the sentiment famously expressed in The New Yorker in 1989, when it ranked Pittsburgh among the world's most beautiful cities, alongside Paris and St. Petersburg, Russia.*

*"If Pittsburgh were situated somewhere in the heart of Europe, tourists would eagerly journey hundreds of miles out of their way to visit it," the magazine said.*

**Josh Noel – Chicago Tribune - 2014**

- *Pittsburgh is a place with a beguiling combination of natural beauty and urban quirkiness. Also, much better-looking, almost like it stole a move from Seattle or Portland. The most striking feature is the rugged topography, which has no obvious equivalent among big cities anywhere in the East. I've never seen it look anything but clean and fresh.*

   **Joel Achenbach – The Washington Post, July 2015**

- *Pittsburgh is a happening place to visit...and move too (2016).*

   **Vogue Magazine**

- *Old school stalwarts mingle with artsy young people, helping to create a city that serves as a canvas for the kind of urban dreams that more crowded and expensive cities can't foster.*

   **Brendan Spiegal – The New York Times, July 2015**

- *Pittsburgh feels busy, it feels alive. Industry has given way to research, health care, education and the arts. Smart people are moving in, or simply moving home. The city feels young again, promising, like a place that has a future, one better than any of its contemporaries.*

   **David Lansel – Huffington Post Travel (2015)**

- *This is the only city in America with an entrance. You slide and slither into most downtowns, passing through gradual layers of ever-more-intensely built-up sprawl, and you do not so much*

*enter the center as realize after you are there that it is all around you. Not Pittsburgh. Pittsburgh is entered with glory and drama.*
**Paul Goldberger – The New York Times – 1988**

- *You talk about an island in the Darwinian sense. Here's a major American city stuck at the end of a series of river valleys, cut off from the rest of country. It is an Eastern European immigrant city — working class, blue collar — that has reinvented itself over the last 10-20 years with this craftsman approach to life that reminds me of cities like Austin, Portland, Oregon and Portland, Maine. I hate to be one of those people who's like 'Pittsburgh is the next big thing,' but I get around more than most people and I'm telling you, Pittsburgh is like the next big thing. The geography lends itself, it's incredibly lush farmland, and inexpensive city with incredible history. They're renovating 100 year old railroad terminals into city markets. They had chefs who left the city because there was no scene and went to LA, they have the talent to be anywhere in America, and they have come back and can afford to open their own places and do what they want. It's very, very exciting. As a student of these things, there's just enough Fortune 500, sports teams, to feed that group. The art community and food community are kind of leading but there's money following them ... why not get a beautiful house on the river? I saw places that are just breathtaking. It's also got the Appalachians running through, so it's got stunning geography. The food scene is cool. Lots of good stuff going on.*
**Andrew Zimmern – TV Host - June 2013**

- *The road from D.C. to Pittsburgh is, well, green...to be honest, it was a haze of emerald and photosynthesis in action. It definitely got rockier. As for Pittsburgh itself, well, it's definitely a "must visit." Like a hipper, organic, authentic version of the cool downtown area near you with the bricks, only they have more bars, better food, and a brilliant arts scene.*
**James Joiner - Esquire Magazine - July 2014**

3

- *Pittsburgh looks fantastic! I've noticed more and more films are using Pittsburgh as a setting, so it must be a great place. Beautiful city. It has more bridges than Venice.*
  **David Letterman and Tom Cruise – David Letterman Show - December 2012**

- *Pittsburgh entered the core of my heart when I was a boy and cannot be torn out.*
  **Andrew Carnegie – Industrialist, Philanthropist**

- *Pittsburgh was even more, vital, more creative, more hungry for culture than New York. Pittsburgh was the birthplace of my writing.*
  **Willa Cather – Pulitzer Prize Winning Author**

- Pittsburgh, the place to be for innovation (2016).
  **Katie Couric – TV Broadcaster - via the New York Times**

- *Driving out of the Fort Pitt Tunnel onto the bridge at night as the skyline explodes in front of you gets me every time. The city is also a hub for art and culture. Between the great theater scene, Frank Lloyd Wright's Fallingwater house, and Pittsburgh native Andy Warhol's museum, there is some great culture to be had. Aside from these, Mount Washington's observation decks offer a great view of the city skyline.*
  **Joe Manginello - Actor – Vanity Fair**

- *I have to tell this story. Oh, my god, if I don't do this nothing else makes sense. I must go to Pittsburgh! I must go to Pittsburgh! I must get funding for this movie.*
  **Emma Watson – Actor – On her return to acting to film Perks of Being a Wallflower**

- *I love Pittsburgh – it's nice and homey. Pittsburgh is home.*
  **Michael Keaton – Actor – Hometown – Coraopolis, Pennsylvania**

- *Pittsburgh: Take one part hipster rejuvenation, two parts industrial character, and mix well. The result is one authentically cool place.*

  **Benjy Hansen-Bundy – GQ Magazine - 2017**

- *Pittsburgh...I found a city that has transformed itself into a vibrant cultural and artistic hub...*

  **Lucas Peterson – The New York Times – 2017**

- *The city has also seen an influx of "boomerangers," Pittsburgh natives or their kids who have returned to their ancestral turf. And new waves of transplants are arriving from Philadelphia, New York and beyond., lured by a quality of life that consistently earns Pittsburgh a perch in the upper reaches of the Economist's annual Global Livability Ranking.*

  **Jody Rosen – Travel & Leisure Magazine – 2016**

- *In fact, Pittsburgh is not just a happening place to visit – increasingly, people, especially New Yorkers, are toying with the idea of moving here.*

  **Stephen Heyman – Vogue Magazine – 2016**

- *The new hot American city*

  **The Today Show**

- *Pittsburgh is beautiful and has great passion.*

  **The Travel Channel**

- *Pittsburgh Wows first-time visitors.*

  **Frommers**

- *Pittsburgh has emerged as a city of beauty and culture.*

  **Lonely Planet**

- *Pittsburgh is a city on the rise.*

  **USA Today Travel**

- *One of the Top Two most beautiful places in America.*
**USA Weekend**

- *This city is on fire.*
**Conde Nast Traveler**

- *One of the most attractive and most livable cities.*
**Rough Guides**

- *Pittsburgh has undergone a stirring renaissance...a cool – dare I say, hip-city.*
**New York Times Travel Guide**

- *Should we all just move to Pittsburgh?*
**Nicole Davis – Brooklyn Based - 2015**

## ACCOLADES

The world's most renowned publications, organizations and companies have also completed their thorough analysis and have found this City of Pittsburgh to be impressive and a model for all cities to follow. Pittsburgh can be said to have received more positive rankings than any major U.S. city. Here are a few (mostly) recent accolades – within the past three to five years. It would reasonable to assume that no other city in the United States can match the praise bestowed below. Being highly regarded by many international and national publications and media sources are nothing new to Pittsburgh and it may actually have the highest overall rankings of any city.

### Living in Pittsburgh
- Pittsburgh: **#1 for jobs (2017)** - Glassdoor
- Pittsburgh: **Top 40 World Cities to Live in (2017)** – The Economist
- Pittsburgh: **Top 3 Cities for an Active Lifestyle (2017)** - Wallethub

- Pittsburgh: **Top 10 Cities with Affordable Housing (2017)** - Wallethub
- Pittsburgh: **Top 3 Cities to Live in (2017) - Wallethub**
- Pittsburgh: **Top 10 Cities to Start Your Career (2017)** – Bankrate.com
- Pittsburgh: **Top City for College Grads to Find a Job (2016)** - Bloomberg
- Pittsburgh: **Top 2 Cities for First-Time Homebuyers (2016)** – Zillow.com
- Pittsburgh: **Best Places to Live (2016)** – Men's Journal Magazine
- Pittsburgh: **Top 5 Most Livable Downtowns (2016)** – Livability.com
- Pittsburgh: **Top 3 Cities for First-Time Homebuyers (2016)** – Zillow.com
- Pittsburgh: **Top 4 Cities for First-Time Homebuyers (2016)** – SmartAsset.com
- Pittsburgh: **Top 25 Cities for Young Families (2016)** - ValuePenguin
- Pittsburgh: **Most Livable Place in the Continental United States** – *The Economist Magazine*
- Pittsburgh: **One of the most Livable Places in the World and Best in the U.S.** – *The Economist Magazine*
- Pittsburgh: **Top 5 Best Cities to Live in the U.S. (2015)** – Money Magazine
- Pittsburgh: **Best City to Live in the Northeast (2015)** – Money Magazine
- Pittsburgh: **One of the World's 11 Best & Most Livable Cities (2015)** – Metropolis Magazine
- Pittsburgh: **Most Livable U.S. City** – Forbes Magazine
- Pittsburgh: **The Most Livable City** – BestPlaces.net
- Pittsburgh: **Most Livable City in the U.S.** – Rand McNally
- Pittsburgh: **Most Livable City in the U.S.** (Twice) – Places Rated Almanac
- Pittsburgh: **Best Cities for Millennials** – Niche, Inc.
- Pittsburgh: **Best Cities for those in their 20's** – Greatest.com

- Pittsburgh: **Top 10 Cities for Techies (2016)** – Huffington Post
- Pittsburgh: **Top 3 Cities for Working Mothers (2016)** – Realtor.com
- Pittsburgh: **Top 10 Safest Cities for Walkers (2017)** – Curb.com
- Pittsburgh: **America's Reborn City (2015)** – Men's Journal Magazine
- Pittsburgh: **Top 5 Trendiest Cities in U.S.** – Realtor.com
- Pittsburgh: **Ten Best Places to Pursue the American Dream** – *The Atlantic Magazine*
- Pittsburgh: **Best Cities to Move to** – BestPlaces.net
- Pittsburgh: **#1 Best City to Relocate to** – CNBC
- Pittsburgh: **Top City for Relocating Families** – Worldwide ERC
- Pittsburgh: **#1 Outdoor Adventure City** – National Geographic
- Pittsburgh: **Best Outdoor Towns** – Outside Magazine
- Pittsburgh: **Top 5 Cities for Obtaining a Mortgage** – Realtor.com
- Pittsburgh: **Best Downtown of Mid-Sized Cities (2015)**– Liveability.com
- Pittsburgh: **Third most secure major city in America** – Farmers Insurance Company
- Pittsburgh: **Third Safest major city in America** – Sperling BestPlaces
- Pittsburgh: **Top 10 Most Walkable U.S. Cities** – MSN City Guides
- Pittsburgh: **Top 20 Safest U.S. Cities** – *Forbes Magazine*
- Pittsburgh: **Top 10 Cities for Homebuyers** – Movoto
- Pittsburgh: **2ⁿᵈ Busiest Millennial Housing Market** – Realtor.com
- Pittsburgh: **Top 20 Most Charming U.S. Cities (2015)** – Travel & Leisure
- Pittsburgh: **Top 4 Cities in the Nation for New Employee Job Growth** - ZipRecruiter
- Pittsburgh: **Fifth most resilient city in the World** – Grosvenor Research of London
- Pittsburgh: **Top 10 Best City for Recreation** – Nerdwallet. Com

- Pittsburgh: **Top 15 best cities for recreation** – WalletHub
- Pittsburgh: **Top 10 cities for telecommuters** – Highspeedinterenet.com
- Pittsburgh: **One of the country's next hipster meccas** – PolicyMic.com
- Pittsburgh: **Smartest City in the United States** – Motovo Real Estate
- Pittsburgh: **One of America's Top Growing Cities** – U-Haul
- Pittsburgh: **2015 - Top 10 Foodie City** – Liveability.com
- Pittsburgh: **Top Romantic Cities in the World (Unexpected)** – *Forbes Magazine*
- Pittsburgh: **Most Romantic City in the U.S.** – Amazon.com
- Pittsburgh: **One of the Top Children's Hospital in the U.S.** – *Parents' Magazine*
- Pittsburgh: **Top 10 most well-read U.S. cities** – Amazon.com
- Pittsburgh: **Top 5 Happiest Cities to work in** – Careerbliss.com
- Pittsburgh: **Top 5 Large City "College Towns"** – WalletHub.com
- Pittsburgh: **Fastest Growing Cities for Technology Jobs** – Dice.com
- Pittsburgh: **Top 5 Cities for Working Moms** – *Forbes Magazine*
- Pittsburgh: **10 Best Cities for Education** – *Parenting Magazine*
- Pittsburgh: **Top 10 Cities for Personal Income Growth** – Portfolio.com
- Pittsburgh: **Top 6 Cities for Job Growth** – US Bureau of Labor Statistics
- Pittsburgh: **5th Best City for an Active Lifestyle** – WalletHub.com
- Pittsburgh: **Top 10 Healthiest Cities** – BestDoctor.com
- Pittsburgh: **7th Healthiest City** – BetterDoctor.com
- Pittsburgh: **Top Cities for Foodies – 2015** – NerdWallet.com
- Pittsburgh: **10 Most Affordable Foodie Cities** – Wallethub
- Pittsburgh: **Top 10 Cities for Beer** – SmartAsset.com

## Affordability of Living in Pittsburgh

- Pittsburgh: **Top 10 Most Affordable Housing Markets** - Wallethub
- Pittsburgh: **Top 5 Most Livable Downtowns (2016)** – Liveability.com
- Pittsburgh: **Most affordable Place to Own a Home in U.S.** – HSH.com (Mortgage Company)
- Pittsburgh: **Most affordable City to Own a Home** – Demographia International Housing Affordability Survey
- Pittsburgh: **Top 5 most affordable cities in regards to housing** – Interest.com
- Pittsburgh: **America's Strongest Housing Markets** – *Forbes Magazine*
- Pittsburgh: **Top 200 Most Affordable Cities in the World** – Mercer Consulting
- Pittsburgh: **Best U.S. Housing Markets** – *Forbes Magazine*
- Pittsburgh: **Best U.S. Housing Markets** – BestPlaces.net
- Pittsburgh: **Best Place to Buy a Home** – Forbes magazine
- Pittsburgh: **Top 20 most affordable cities in the United States** – *Forbes Magazine*
- Pittsburgh: **America's Best Bang-For-The Buck Cities** – *Forbes Magazine*
- Pittsburgh: **Most affordable U.S. cities** – BestPlaces.net
- Pittsburgh: **Top 8 Cities where Millennials won't break the bank** – PolicyMic.com
- Pittsburgh: **One of the most affordable big cities in the U.S.** – The Simple Dollar
- Pittsburgh: **Top 5 Cities for Wallet Wellness** – Cardhub.com

## Retiring in Pittsburgh

- Pittsburgh: **Top 10 Surprisingly Best Places to Retire (2016)** – Kiplinger Magazine
- Pittsburgh: **Top 25 Best Places to Retire (2015)** – Forbes Magazine
- Pittsburgh: **8th Best Metro Area to Retire (2015)** – Cities Affordable/Health Study

- Pittsburgh: **Cheapest Places Where You Will Want to Retire** – Kiplinger Magazine
- Pittsburgh: **Fifth Best Place to Retire** – Livability.com
- Pittsburgh: **Top Five Places to Retire on Social Security Alone** – Yahoo Finance
- Pittsburgh: **Top Places to Retire for under $40,000** – *US News & World Report*
- Pittsburgh: **#1 City where Boomers Should Retire** – Movoto Real Estate
- Pittsburgh: **25 Best Places to Retire** – CNN Money
- Pittsburgh: **Best Places to Retire** – *Forbes Magazine*
- Pittsburgh: **One of the most Affordable Cities to Retire** – Livability.com

## Visiting Pittsburgh

- Pittsburgh: **Top 5 Places in the World to Visit (2017)** – Harpers-Bizarre
- Pittsburgh: **Pittsburgh Airport/Airport of the Year (2017)** – Air Transport World Magazine
- Pittsburgh: **Top Destinations on the Rise (2016)** – TripAdvisor
- Pittsburgh: **#1 City for Beer Lovers (2016)** – The Beer Institute
- Pittsburgh: **Top 10 U.S. Travel Destinations** – TripAdvisor
- Pittsburgh: **Best Places to Visit in 2016** – Travel & Leisure Magazine
- Pittsburgh: **Hollywood East** – Entertainment Weekly
- Pittsburgh: **Hollywood of the East** - CNN
- Pittsburgh: **Top 10 Beer Cities** - InfoGroup
- Pittsburgh: **#3 of Places to Go in 2015** – Conde Nast Magazine
- Pittsburgh: **One of the best All-American vacations for 2014** – *The Travel Channel*
- Pittsburgh: **One of the Top World-wide Destinations of 2013** – Jetsetter.com
- Pittsburgh: **#1 Food City in United States** – Zagat
- Pittsburgh: **The Next Big Food Town** – Bon Appetit Magazine
- Pittsburgh: **Top 10 Best Bed and Breakfast Cities** – BedeandBreakfast.com

- Pittsburgh: **Best Traditional Amusement Park (Kennywood)** – National Amusement Park Historical Association
- Pittsburgh: **Top 3 Cities for Nightlife** – *Woman's Health Magazine/Yelp*
- Pittsburgh: **Top Ten Most Beautiful Places in America** – USAToday
- Pittsburgh: **Prettiest Cities in the World** – Huffington Post
- Pittsburgh: **Best Skylines in the U.S.** – Destination360.com
- Pittsburgh: **Best U.S. Skylines** – BestPlaces.net
- Pittsburgh: **Top 25 World's Best Skylines** – Skyscraperpage.com
- Pittsburgh: **Best Skylines in the World** – Deserio.com
- Pittsburgh: **Best Skylines of the World** – Blogspot.com
- Pittsburgh: **#5 in America's Best Riverfronts** – USA Today
- Pittsburgh: **Definitely a must visit** – *Esquire Magazine*
- Pittsburgh: **One of the most Underrated Cities** – Conde Nast Traveler
- Pittsburgh: **Top 15 Best Affordable Destinations in the USA** – *US News & World Report*
- Pittsburgh: **The Ultimate Urban Hike in the U.S.** – Yahoo Travel
- Pittsburgh: **Best Views in America** – *Travel + Leisure Magazine*
- Pittsburgh: **Most exciting place in Pennsylvania** – Movoto
- Pittsburgh: **One of America's most stunning views** – *USA Today*
- Pittsburgh: **America's best baseball park: PNC Park** – ESPN
- Pittsburgh: **Best ballpark in the U.S.** – TripAdvisor.com
- Pittsburgh: **Top 5 Iconic Ballparks** – Roadtrippers
- Pittsburgh: **Top 5 Rising Star Destinations** – Gogobot.com
- Pittsburgh: **Top 10 Places you Should Visit** – IndependentTraveler.com
- Pittsburgh: **Top 10 Fun City** – American City Business Journals
- Pittsburgh: **One of America's Top Art Destinations** – *AmericanStyle Managzine*
- Pittsburgh: **#1 Sports City in the nation** – Sporting News
- Pittsburgh: **Favorite U.S. Travel Destination** – Peter Greenberg Worldwide

- Pittsburgh: **Favorite U.S. Destination** – Lonely Planet Travel Guide
- Pittsburgh: **Best City to celebrate St. Patrick's Day** - Niche.com
- Pittsburgh: **Best City for Beer Lovers** - Redfin

## Doing Business in Pittsburgh

- Pittsburgh: **#1 City – Small Business Sector (2017)** – Main St. Index
- Pittsburgh: **Next Tech City (2017)** – MetLife Investment Management
- Pittsburgh: **Most Undervalued U.S. City (2017)** – Smartasset.com
- Pittsburgh: **Top 10 Great Cities for Starting a Business** – *Kiplinger Magazine*
- Pittsburgh: **Top 10 Cities for Venture Capital** – MoneyTree.com
- Pittsburgh: **The 15 Hottest Cities for 2015** – Business Insider
- Pittsburgh: **One of the Best Cities for Young Entrepreneurs** – Under30ceo.com
- Pittsburgh: **Top 15 cities for start-up capital investment** – The National Venture Capital Association
- Pittsburgh: **Fastest Growing Cities for Technology Jobs** – Dice.com
- Pittsburgh: **Top 5 Cities to Launch a New Business** – *Forbes Magazine*
- Pittsburgh: **Best Commercial Real Estate Markets** - Moodys
- Pittsburgh: **Fastest Recovering U.S. City** – BestPlaces.net
- Pittsburgh: **Top 25 U.S. Economic Powerhouses** – Bureau of Economic Analysis
- Pittsburgh: **Top 10 Emerging Tech Markets** – Jones Lang LaSalle
- Pittsburgh: **Top 10 Healthiest Retail Markets** – Chainlink Retail
- Pittsburgh: **Top 12 Cities for Per Capita Growth** – US Bureau of Economic Analysis

- Pittsburgh: **Top 25 Cities for Small Business** – Business Journals
- Pittsburgh: **Top 5 Cities for Working Moms** – *Forbes Magazine*
- Pittsburgh: **Ten Best Places to Pursue the American Dream** – *The Atlantic Magazine*
- Pittsburgh: **Top 3 Best Opportunity City** – Forbes
- Pittsburgh: **Top City for Employee Satisfaction** – Inc.com
- Pittsburgh: **Best Cities to Move to** – BestPlaces.net
- Pittsburgh: **#1 Best City to Relocate to** – CNBC
- Pittsburgh: **Top City for Relocating Families** – Worldwide ERC
- Pittsburgh: **Top 10 Cities of the Future (2015)** – fDi Magazine

For more of Pittsburgh's rankings, please visit:
Visitpittsburgh.com/media/press-kit/pittsburgh

# Chapter 2

# VISITING PITTSBURGH TRANSPORTATION AND HOTELS

## TRANSPORTATION – GETTING TO PITTSBURGH

You can travel to Pittsburgh via air, train, bus or boat:

### Pittsburgh International Airport

Located approximately 20 miles west from Downtown Pittsburgh, Pittsburgh International is one of the Top 10 airports in the United States in land size and is often rated as one of the best airports. In 2017, it was rated as *Airport of the Year* by *Air Transport World Magazine*, the first time a U.S. airport has received the honor. It is served by major airlines, as well as discount carriers, that fly to 54 destinations (the airport has over 170 non-stop flights). As of this writing, Pittsburgh International has direct flights to European destinations, such as France, Germany and Iceland, as well as Canada, Mexico, and the Caribbean. The airport is equipped with many amenities, including an AirMall. The drive from the airport to Downtown or the suburbs is served by major highway systems. The airport is undergoing a $1.1 billion project to construct a new landside terminal and renovation of the airside terminal, including expanded security checkpoints and a new baggage system.

www.pitairport.com

## Amtrak – Union Station – Pittsburgh

Union Station, also known as Pennsylvania or Penn Station, is a historic train station in Downtown Pittsburgh. The primary Amtrak routes are the *Pennsylvanian*, which is starts in New York City, travels through Philadelphia and ends in Pittsburgh and the *Capitol Limited*, which begins in Washington, DC, travels to Pittsburgh and ends in Chicago. Connecting travel is available.

www.amtrak.com

## Greyhound Bus Line – Pittsburgh

Located in Downtown Pittsburgh, the Greyhound station is part of the Grant Street Transportation Center. All destinations are served from this location, via direct routes or through connections.

greyhound.com

## Megabus – Pittsburgh

The Megabus line centers its operations of arriving and departing passengers in Downtown Pittsburgh at the David L. Lawrence Convention Center (next to the Greyhound Station). Megabus travels to and from 15 cities from Pittsburgh.

megabus.com

## American Cruise Lines

Travel to Pittsburgh on a riverboat cruise. Pittsburgh is the final stop on the Ohio River Tour that travels from St. Louis to Pittsburgh.

americancruiselines.com

**Other Airports:**

**Allegheny County Airport**

Located just four miles southeast of Pittsburgh, the airport is the fifth busiest in Pennsylvania. The airport was formerly Pittsburgh's primary metro airport until 1952. The airport serves commercial, corporate and private traffic. The airport also has the capabilities to accommodate large commercial jets.

pitairport.com

**Arnold Palmer Regional Airport**

Located in Latrobe, Pennsylvania and named after the town's native son – golfing great Arnold Palmer – the airport is 33 miles southeast of Pittsburgh. The airport is served by a discount airline.

palmerairport.com

**Transportation in Downtown Pittsburgh and the suburbs:**

**Port Authority of Allegheny County**

Downtown Pittsburgh and surrounding suburbs is served by the Port Authority of Allegheny County. The Port Authority or PAT provides bus, subway and incline (funicular) transportation. PAT operates approximately 700 buses that provide service in Allegheny County and portions of surrounding counties. PAT also operates a light-rail subway system (known as the "T") that covers 26 miles from Downtown Pittsburgh. In addition, it operates the Duquesne Incline, which transports passengers from Mount Washington to the Downtown area.

portauthority.org

**Taxi/Bus Systems**

Pittsburgh is served by several taxi service companies, as well as Super Shuttle, Uber (including driverless taxis) and Lyft. Additional bus lines are available that transport passengers to surrounding counties. See local tour information in the next chapter.

pghtrans.com

## Traveling by Car

Pittsburgh is served by many major highways and interstates. Mapquest.com or GPS

## Duquesne Incline

If you want to see what *USA Today Weekend Magazine* calls one of the "10 most beautiful views in America", the historic Duquesne Incline is a must. Ride to the top of Pittsburgh's Mount Washington and enjoy a spectacular panorama of Pittsburgh and its three rivers from the Observation Deck. Historical exhibits are also viewable in the Incline Shop.

The Duquesne Incline is located on West Carson Street near Station Square and Pittsburgh's Southside.
- 1197 West Carson St.
  Pittsburgh, PA 15219
- 412-381-1665

## Monongahela Incline

Known as the Mon Incline - the Monongahela Incline is the oldest continuously operating funicular railway in the U.S. It's been in operation since May 28, 1870, and has since then transported millions of passengers. The Monongahela Incline overlook provides one of the world's great cityscapes. Tourists enjoy a skyline view, while riding one of the few remaining inclines in the country (two in Pittsburgh – Duquesne Incline). The inclines are a great way to travel to the top of Mount Washington or to reach Downtown Pittsburgh and Station Square.
- Stations: West Carson Street (Southside at Station Square)
  Grandview Avenue (Mount Washington)
- 412-381-1665

# HOTELS

Pittsburgh has experienced a hotel building boom over the past few years and the trend is continuing. You will easily find all hotel levels throughout the city and most are within walking distance of many major attractions. Here are some of the more well-known establishments, but be sure to check the link below for all of the hotels available:

**Omni William Penn**
- 530 William Penn Place
  Downtown
- 412-281-7100

**Hotel Monaco – Klimpton**
- 620 William Penn Place
  Downtown
- 855-338-3837

**Embassy Suites by Hilton**
- 535 Smithfield Street
  Downtown
- 412-338-2200

**Wyndam Grand Pittsburgh**
- 600 Commonwealth Place
  Downtown
- 412-391-4600

**Westin Convention Center Pittsburgh**
- 1000 Penn Avenue
  Downtown
- 412-281-3700

**Drury Plaza Hotel Pittsburgh**
- 745 Grant Street
  Downtown

- 412-281-2900

## Fairmont Pittsburgh
- 510 Market Street
  Downtown
- 888-270-6647

## Renaissance Pittsburgh
- 107 Sixth Street
  Downtown
- 412-562-1200

## Marriott Pittsburgh City Center
- 112 Washington Place
  Downtown
- 412-471-4000

## Doubletree Hotel & Suites Pittsburgh
- One Bigelow Square
  Downtown
- 412-281-5800

## Sheraton Pittsburgh – Station Square
- 300 West Station Square Drive
  Station Square – Southside
- 412-261-2000

*The William Penn Hotel in Pittsburgh... was the place where Champagne Music was born.*

**Lawrence Welk – Famous Band Leader and Television Personality**

**For a listing of all hotels available, please visit: visitpittsburgh.com/ hotels-resorts/**

# Chapter 3

# TOURING PITTSBURGH

The following is a breakdown of the sites to see in the Pittsburgh area, information about the venue, their general location in the city and their address and phone number. Website links are not generally provided, since a quick "Google" or "Yahoo" search will easily lead you to each venue's current website or go to visitpittsburgh.com

For a map of downtown Pittsburgh and other information, please visit downtownpittsburgh.com

## TOURISM

The City of Pittsburgh combines an incredible skyline with beautiful topography, all within the confines of *America's most Livable City*. The city is a combination of friendly people, great food, deep history, unmatched culture and exciting sports. Drive through its front door – the Fort Pitt Tunnel – and experience one of the world's most amazing views. Take a ride on one of the few remaining funiculars (cable cars) in the country to the top of Mount Washington and experience what *USA Today* called one of "America's Most Stunning Views."

- Pittsburgh: **Top 5 Places in the World to Visit (2017)** – Harpers-Bazaar
- Pittsburgh: **Top Destinations on the Rise (2016)** – TripAdvisor
- Pittsburgh: **Top 10 U.S. Travel Destinations** – TripAdvisor

- Pittsburgh: **Best Places to Visit in 2016** – Travel & Leisure Magazine
- Pittsburgh: **#3 of Places to Go in 2015** – Conde Nast Magazine
- Pittsburgh: **One of the best All-American vacations for 2014** – *The Travel Channel*
- Pittsburgh: **One of the Top World-wide Destinations of 2013** – Jetsetter.com

Some of more unique attractions include, The National Aviary, Kennywood Park, St. Anthony's Chapel, The Carnegie Museums and Andy Warhol Museum, The Gateway Clipper Fleet, the Duquesne and Monongahela Inclines, The Fort Pitt Museum, The Pittsburgh Zoo and Aquarium, the view from Mount Washington and the view upon entering the city from the Fort Pitt Tunnels. This is but a few of the entertainment and historical attractions that are described in the following chapters.

## TOURS

### Gateway Clipper Fleet

Take to Pittsburgh's Three Rivers for an incredible sightseeing tour of one of the most beautiful cities in the world on six large riverboats. An incredible skyline outlined by architecture and natural landscapes, create a tour that you don't want to miss. Dining cruises feature delicious buffets prepared by an award winning Executive Chef. Gateway Clipper also offers shuttling services for North Shore sporting events. For over 50 years the Gateway Clipper Fleet has been sailing the Three Rivers hosting Pittsburgh Sightseeing and Dining Cruises. The cruise line is located in Station Square on Pittsburgh's Southside.

- 350 W. Station Square Drive
  Pittsburgh, PA 15219
- 412-355-7980

### Molly's Trolleys

Molly's Trolleys provides sightseeing services on 1920's style fleet of trolleys with 30-passenger seating capacity. The fleet is equipped with panoramic windows and includes period-style interior woodwork, and brass railings. Molly's Trolleys also provides shuttling services. The fleet is located in Station Square on Pittsburgh's Southside.

- 125 W. Station Square Drive
  Pittsburgh, PA 15219
- 412-281-2085

## Just Ducky Tours

Just Ducky Tours takes riders on Pittsburgh's only adventure through the city on land and water. Enjoy the tour as military-style craft tour the city, while taking you from "sea to shore."

The tour is located in Station Square on Pittsburgh's South Side.

- 125 W. Station Square Drive
  Pittsburgh, PA 15219
- 412-402-3825

## Pittsburgh Tours & More

Take a tour of Pittsburgh's movie, beer, sports or food scene. See where numerous movies were filmed in "Hollywood of the East," (The Dark Knight Rises, Perks of Being a Wallflower, Flashdance, Next Three Days, Inspector Gadget, Abduction, Jack Reacher and many others). A portion of the proceeds goes to the Pittsburgh Film Office.

- 1825 Liverpool Street
  Pittsburgh, PA 15233
- 412-323-4709

## Pittsburgh Tour Company

The Pittsburgh Tour Company's Double Decker tour offers Pittsburgh's only Hop On/Hop Off Tour. The tour uses historic red Double Decker Tour Buses from London. Tour guides lead you on a guided tour of Pittsburgh's favorite areas for entertainment, shopping, restaurants, museums, bars, stadiums and architecture. There are 21 stops for you to Hop Off and then resume the tour soon thereafter.

The tour company is located in the SouthSide Works shopping district on Pittsburgh's Southside.
- 495 S. 27th Street
  Pittsburgh, PA 15203
- 412-381-8687

**Downtown Pittsburgh Walking Tours**

The Pittsburgh History and Landmarks Foundation sponsors Downtown walking tours from May through October. In addition, there are other local tours from April through November.
- 412-471-5808 – Ext. 527
- Phlf.org

**Pittsburgh Party Pedaler**

A charter service 16-person Dutch-made bike that tours interesting parts of Pittsburgh.
- 1825 Liverpool Street
  Pittsburgh, PA 15233
- 412-228-7476

**For more information on tours, please visit: visitpittsburgh.com**

# Chapter 4

# PITTSBURGH'S CULTURAL ATTRACTIONS

## CULTURAL ATTRACTIONS - MUSEUMS

### Carnegie Museum of Natural History

The Carnegie Museum's dinosaur collection is world famous and includes the first T-Rex ever discovered. The Carnegie is ranked as one of the Top five natural history museums in the country and includes over 20 galleries, including: Hall of Egypt, Dinosaurs in Their Time, Halls of African and North American Wildlife, Hall of Artic Life, Hall of American Indians, Halls of Architecture and Sculpture, Halls of Botany and Geology, Hall of Minerals and Gems and Gallery of Gems and Jewelry. In total, the museum controls a collection of 21 million objects and scientific specimen. The museum also operates a nearby research center known as the Powdermill Nature Reserve. The Museum is located in the heart of Pittsburgh's university district, known as Oakland. The Carnegie Museum of Art is adjacent.

- 4400 Forbes Ave.
  Pittsburgh, PA 15213
- 412-622-3131

## Carnegie Science Center

The Carnegie Science Center includes four floors of incredible experiences, such as Roboworld – the country's largest permanent robotics exhibit, which also includes the Robot Hall-of-Fame, featuring Hollywood's most famous robots. The Center also features the Buhl Planetarium, the Buhl Skywatch Observatory and the International Space Station exhibit – SpacePlace. You'll be amazed by the famous Miniature Railroad & Village and hundreds of hands-on exhibits, as well as featured traveling exhibits. Tour the Cold War-era submarine USS Requin, which participated in classified defense and scientific missions and view a documentary or movie on the incredible screen in the Rangos Omnimax Theater.

The Center also includes the Highmark SportsWorks®, which is an interactive facility that combines science and sports. Thirty exhibits in all, including a 24-foot Rock Wall, You-Yo, and the Physics of Sports.
- One Allegheny Ave.
  Pittsburgh, PA 15212-5850
- (412) 237-3400

## Carnegie Museum of Art

The Carnegie Museum of Art is a museum of contemporary art with more than 30,000 objects including: paintings, sculpture, drawings, prints, photographs, architectural casts, models, film and visual arts. Since the Carnegie International began in 1896, the Carnegie has specialized in collecting what they term the "Old Masters of Tomorrow." This Museum of fine art is also considered by many as the first museum of contemporary arts.

The Carnegie Museum of Art is located in Pittsburgh's Oakland section and adjacent to the Carnegie Museum of Natural History.
- 4400 Forbes Avenue
  Pittsburgh, PA 15213
- 412-622-3131

## Andy Warhol Museum

One of the world's most famous artists is from Pittsburgh – Andy Warhol. The official Andy Warhol Museum is dedicated to his work and is administered by the Carnegie Museum system. Per the Museum - "The art collection includes 900 paintings; approximately 100 sculptures; nearly 2,000 works on paper; more than 1,000 published and unique prints; and 4,000 photographs. The collection also features wallpaper and books by Warhol, covering the entire range of his work from all periods, and includes student work from the 1940s, 1950s drawings, commercial illustrations and sketchbooks; 1960s Pop paintings of consumer products (Campbell's Soup Cans), celebrities (Liz, Jackie, Marilyn, Elvis), Disasters and Electric Chairs; portrait paintings (Mao), Skull paintings and the abstract Oxidations from the 1970s; and works from the 1980s such as The Last Supper, Raphael I-6.99 and collaborative paintings made with younger artists such as Jean-Michel Basquiat and Francesco Clemente. Drawings by Warhol's mother Julia Warhola are also included in the art collection. The film & video collection includes 60 feature films, 200 of Warhol's Screen Tests, and more than 4,000 videos. The museum exhibits Warhol's film and video work on a regular basis in its galleries. The Warhol archives consist mainly of Warhol's papers and other materials from his estate. This includes source materials for his art (such as photographs, newspapers and magazines); a portion of his personal collection of thousands of collectibles, books, and ephemera; 610 *Time Capsules* (a work of art assembled from archival materials from the artist's daily life); a nearly complete run of *Interview* magazine; more than 3,000 audiotapes; and clothing, scripts, diaries, and correspondence." The Museum is located on Pittsburgh's North Shore.
- 117 Sandusky Street
  Pittsburgh, PA 15212
- 412-237-8300

**Heinz History Center** (in association with the Smithsonian Institution)

The Senator John Heinz History Center is Pennsylvania's largest history museum and is an affiliate of the Smithsonian Institution. The Museum celebrates more than 250 years of Western Pennsylvania history on six floors and 370,000 square feet of exhibit space.

Permanent and long-term exhibits appeal to a wide variety of audiences and fill the Museum's six floors. Pittsburgh played a major role in the French & Indian War and the Museum features exhibits in relation to the first "World War." Come see how a young George Washington visited the region just before the British and the French battled for control of America's greatest prize...Pittsburgh. From George Washington's first adventures in the region during the French & Indian War to Pittsburgh's greatest stories - all are told at the History Center. Exhibits include: Clash of Empires (French & Indian War), From Slavery to Freedom, Lewis & Clark, Pittsburgh: A Tradition of Innovation and Kidsburgh. The Museum also houses a library and achieve, as well as a conservation center.

Pittsburgh: A Tradition of Innovation, a two-story, long-term exhibition, which spans more than 16,000 square-feet, celebrates the Pittsburgh region's contribution to art, industry, medicine, sports, technology and education. These exhibits depict how people and inventions that have changed the way we "live, work and play."

Pittsburgh's Lost Steamboat: Treasures of the Arabia, a Pittsburgh-built boat that sank in the Missouri River and was excavated 150 years later with nearly a million perfectly-preserved objects is an incredible exhibit.

The Heinz History Center is located in Pittsburgh's Strip District and just minutes from Downtown.
- 1212 Smallman St.
  Pittsburgh, PA 15222
- 412-454-6000

## Fort Pitt Museum and Fort Pitt Blockhouse

This is where the West began. The Fort Pitt Museum, located in historic Point State Park in downtown Pittsburgh, is a two-floor, 12,000-square-foot museum that presents the story of Western Pennsylvania's essential role during the French & Indian War, the American Revolution, and as the birthplace of Pittsburgh. Visit the oldest building in Pittsburgh, an actual blockhouse of the mighty Fort Pitt. Exhibits include: Fort Pitt: Keystone of the Frontier and Daily Life of for 18th Century Residents in the Ohio Country.

The Museum and Blockhouse are located in Point State Park – Downtown.
- Point State Park
  601 Commonwealth Place
  Pittsburgh, PA 15222
- 412-281-9284

## Frick Art & Historical Center

Per the Museum: "The Frick Pittsburgh is a museum located on five acres of beautifully landscaped lawns and gardens. Tour the Henry Clay Frick family home, Clayton—one of the best preserved Gilded Age mansions in America. Enjoy masterpieces of European art and changing exhibitions in the art museum and explore the collection of historic cars and carriages"

The Museum is located in Point Breeze - Pittsburgh's East End.
- 7227 Reynold Street
  Pittsburgh, PA 15208
- 412-371-0600

## St. Anthony's Chapel

Saint Anthony's Chapel is home to the largest collection of publicly venerable Christian relics – 5,000 in total – in the world outside of the Vatican. This incredible, must see chapel is a piece of Europe in the United States.

St. Anthony's Chapel is located in Pittsburgh's Troy Hill section, near the North Shore.

- 1704 Harpster Street
  Pittsburgh, PA 15212
- 412-231-2994

## Nationality Rooms at the Cathedral of Learning

The Nationality Rooms are located on the University of Pittsburgh's main campus and are a collection of 30 classrooms in the University of Pittsburgh's impressive Cathedral of Learning. The classrooms are a historical landmark and are elaborately decorated in 30 ethnic styles. The Cathedral of Learning is a national historic landmark.

The Cathedral is located in the Oakland section of Pittsburgh near the Carnegie Museums.

- 4200 Fifth Avenue
  Pittsburgh, PA 15260
- 412-624-6000

## Pittsburgh Observatories

### *Allegheny Observatory*

The Allegheny Observatory is a research institution and operated by the Department of Physics and Astronomy at the University of Pittsburgh. The facility is listed on the National Register of Historical Places and is designated as a Pennsylvania state and Pittsburgh History and Landmarks Foundation historic landmark. The main active research pursuit at the Allegheny Observatory involves detection of extrasolar planets. Tours are available.

The Observatory is located in Riverview Park near Pittsburgh's North Shore.

- 159 Riverview Avenue
  Pittsburgh, PA 15214
- 412-321-2400

## *Buhl Observatory*

The Buhl Observatory is located in the Carnegie Science Center and offers celestial viewing to the public in the Sky Watch program.

The Carnegie Science Center is located on Pittsburgh's North Shore.
- One Allegheny Avenue
  Pittsburgh, PA 15212
- 412-237-3400
- 724-444-6944

## Soldiers and Sailors Memorial Hall and Museum

Soldiers and Sailors Memorial Hall and Museum is a National Register of Historic Places landmark and is the largest memorial in the United States dedicated solely to honoring all branches of military veterans and service personnel. The Memorial houses rare and one-of-a-kind exhibits that span the eras from the Civil War to the present day conflicts.

In the 1890's, the museum was created by the Grand Army of the Republic to honor American Civil War veterans. The Memorial today represents all branches of the service and honors both career and citizen soldiers who have served the United States throughout its history.

The Museum is located in the Oakland section of Pittsburgh near the Carnegie Museums.
- 4141 Fifth Avenue
  Pittsburgh, PA 15213
- 412-621-4253

## USS Requin Submarine Museum

The USS Requin is a Cold-War era submarine docked at the Carnegie Science Center. Take a tour of the submarine, which participated in classified defense and scientific missions.

The Carnegie Science Center is located on Pittsburgh's North Shore.
* One Allegheny Ave.
  Pittsburgh, PA 15212-5850
* (412) 237-3400

## Bayernhof Music Museum

Bayernhof Music Museum features a major collection of automated musical instruments from the 19th and 20th centuries. The museum is housed in a German-style mansion situated on an 18-acre, dramatic overlook some 540 feet above the Allegheny River Valley.

The museum is located in the Pittsburgh suburb of O'Hara, not far from the North Shore.
* 225 St. Charles Place
  Pittsburgh, PA 15215
* 412-782-4231

## Mattress Factory

A world-renowned museum of contemporary art, the Mattress Factory uses "site-specific installations in unique spaces."

The museum is located in Pittsburgh's historic Mexican War Streets near the North Shore.
* 500 Sampsonia Way
  Pittsburgh, PA 15212
* 412-231-3169

## Photo Antiquities Museum

The museum is dedicated to photography and its history. The museum houses equipment and images from as early as 1839. The museum features Civil War and Native American photos, as well as many other rare images.

The museum is located near Pittsburgh's North Shore.
- 531 East Ohio Street
Pittsburgh, PA 15212
- 412-231-7881

### Kelso Museum of Near Eastern Archaeology

An impressive collection of Near Eastern and Palestinian artifacts and pottery. The museum is located in the eastern section of Pittsburgh.
- 616 North Highland Avenue
Pittsburgh, PA 15206
- 412-362-5610

### Kerr Memorial Museum

A restored Queen Ann house preserved to show how upper middle-class families lived. The house depicts the Kerr household during the period of 1890 to 1910. The museum is on the U.S. National Register of Historic Places.
- 402 Delaware Avenue
Oakmont, PA 15139
- 412-826-9295

**For more information on local museums and attractions, please visit: visitpittsburgh.com**


## THE PERFORMING ARTS

According to Americans for the Arts, Pittsburgh ranks #1 in total direct spending on arts and culture.

### Pittsburgh Broadway Series

The Broadway Series features new touring Broadway shows, as well as "revivals" direct from Broadway. The Series includes regular Tony Award winning performances, classic shows and other events. The

Broadway series is primarily showcased at the beautiful Benedum Center for Performing Arts in the Cultural District.
- 237 Seventh Street
  Pittsburgh, PA 15222
- 412-456-6666

## Pittsburgh Symphony Orchestra (PSO)

The world-touring and highly acclaimed Orchestra is known to perform music at the highest level of expression and artistic excellence. Classical performances are a staple of the annual season, but special concerts and performances are also on the schedule. The Orchestra performs at one of the country's best venues, Heinz Hall for the Performing Arts in the Cultural District.
- 600 Penn Avenue
  Pittsburgh, PA 15222
- 412-392-4900

## Pittsburgh Ballet Theatre

The Ballet prides itself on innovation and excellence and is often considered one of the most exciting companies in the country. Classical, new and seasonal favorites complete the annual performances. The Ballet performs at the Benedum Center for the Performing Arts in the Cultural District.
- 7th Street and Penn Avenue
  Pittsburgh, PA 15222
- 412-456-6666

## Pittsburgh Opera

The Opera often draws national and international attention for its highest standards of artistic excellence. Since 1939, the classics and the new fill the schedule on an annual basis. The Opera performs at the elegant Benedum Center for the Performing Arts.

- 7<sup>th</sup> Street and Penn Avenue
  Pittsburgh, PA 15222
- 412-456-6666

## Pittsburgh Civic Light Opera

The CLO is a musical theater company dedicated to developing new musicals and products for Broadway and regional audiences. The CLO has developed Broadway shows and garnered numerous Tony Award nominations. The Civic Light Opera's excellent schedule of performances can be viewed at the Benedum Center for the Performing Arts in the Cultural District and in the CLO Cabaret Theater.

- 237 7<sup>th</sup> Street
  Pittsburgh, PA 15222
- 412-456-6666

## Pittsburgh Conservatory Theater Company

The Conservatory includes both theater and dance performances and has included 18 major productions and over 200 performances per year. The performances are held at the new Pittsburgh Playhouse in Downtown.

- Forbes Avenue
  Pittsburgh, PA 15222
- 412-391-4100

For more information on cultural events, please visit: trustarts.org

Chapter 5

# ENTERTAINMENT AND FAMILY FUN IN PITTSBURGH

## EDUCATIONAL AND FAMILY FUN

### Pittsburgh Zoo & Aquarium

The Pittsburgh Zoo & PPG Aquarium is situated on 77-acres and features approximately 4,000 mammals, birds, reptiles, fish, and amphibians from across the globe. The Zoo features animals in their naturalistic habitats and native ranges. The Zoo habitats include: African Savanna, Asian Forest, Tropical Rainforest, The Islands, Water's Edge, PPG Aquarium and Kid's Kingdom.

The Pittsburgh Zoo and PPG Aquarium are located in Pittsburgh's Highland Park area.
- One Wild Place
  Pittsburgh, PA 15206
- 412-665-3640

### National Aviary

The official "Bird Zoo" of the United States, the National Aviary is home to more than 500 birds and 150 species. Dedicated exclusively to birds, the National Aviary also cares for species threatened or endangered in the wild.

The Nation's premier Bird Zoo includes Penguin Point, which provides close-up views of swimming penguins and large walk-through exhibits of free-flying birds. Exhibits include: Tropical Rainforest, Grasslands, Wetlands, Cloud Forest, Eagle Hall and Condor Court. You can also visit FliteZone Theater – which offers daily shows and Sky Deck – which allows guests to view birds of prey in flying demonstrations. The Aviary features species never seen in zoos. The National Aviary is located on Pittsburgh's North Shore.

- Allegheny Commons West
  Pittsburgh, PA 15212
- 412-323-7235

## Phipps Conservatory & Botanical Gardens

Discover nature in the heart of city at the Phipps Conservatory. The Conservatory is known for seasonal flower shows, incredible indoor and outdoor gardens, sustainable architecture, Butterfly Forest and a renowned café.

The Phipps Conservatory is located in Pittsburgh's Schenley Park (Oakland).

- One Schenley Park
  Pittsburgh, PA 15213
- 412-622-6914

## Pittsburgh Botanic Gardens

The Pittsburgh Botanic Garden is a world-class botanical garden in the Pittsburgh suburbs. The garden spans across a total of 460 acres, making it among the top 10 largest American botanical gardens. The Pittsburgh Botanic Garden will be the only botanic garden in the United States built on reclaimed land and fits perfectly with Pittsburgh's growing "green" reputation. Per the website: The Garden is comprised of 18 distinct gardens, five diverse woodland experiences, an enhanced visitor's center, an amphitheater for outdoor concerts and performances, a celebration center and a center for botanic research. The Pittsburgh Botanic Garden's mission is to inspire people to grow through immersion in a world of natural outdoor wonder to nourish mind, body and spirit.

- 799 Pinkerton Run Road
  Oakdale, PA 15071
- 412-444-4464

## Pittsburgh Children's Museum

The Museum continues to delight and inspire children of all ages with exhibits based on subjects such as, Mr. Rogers and Us, Daniel Tiger's Neighborhood, Backyard, Garage, Attic, Workshop, Nursery and they include plenty of "Real Stuff" exhibits. The Museum also includes a Theater and Makeshop.

The Pittsburgh Children's Museum is located on Pittsburgh's North Shore – near the National Aviary.

- 10 Children's Way
  Allegheny Square
  Pittsburgh, PA 15212
- 412-322-5058

## Robot Hall of Fame

The Robot Hall-of-Fame is located in the Carnegie Science Center and features Hollywood's most famous robots. Some of the inductees include R2-D2, C-3PO, Lt. Commander Data, Wall-E, Hal, Robby – the Robot and the Mars Pathfinder. Per the website: The Robot Hall of Fame recognizes excellence in robotics technology worldwide and honors the fictional and real robots that have inspired and made breakthrough accomplishments in robotics. The Robot Hall of Fame was created by Carnegie Mellon University to call attention to the increasing contributions of robots to society.

The Carnegie Science Center is located on Pittsburgh's North Shore.

- One Allegheny Ave.
  Pittsburgh, PA 15212-5850
- (412) 237-3400

## The Toonseum

The Toonseum is a Museum of Cartoon Art and devoted exclusively to the cartoon arts. ToonSeum is one of only three museums dedicated to cartoon art in the United States.

The museum is located in Downtown Pittsburgh (Cultural District).
- 945 Liberty Avenue
  Pittsburgh, PA 15222
- 412-232-0199

## Kennywood Park

Kennywood Park, America's #1 traditional amusement park, is a historic landmark and located just a short drive from Downtown. Founded in 1898, the Park includes seven world-class roller coasters, three water rides, thrill rides, classic and dark rides, live shows, exciting games, Kiddie Land and great food.

Kennywood is located in Pittsburgh's West Mifflin suburb.
- 4800 Kennywood Blvd.
  West Mifflin, PA 15122
- 412-461-0500

## Sandcastle Water Park

Pittsburgh's waterpark entices you to stroll along the Boardwalk and enjoy 15 waterslide attractions, the Lazy River, Wave Pool and Children's Area.

Sandcastle is located in Pittsburgh's Waterfront shopping district (Homestead).
- 1000 Sandcastle Dr.
  Homestead, PA 15120
- 412-461-3694

## The Western Pennsylvania Sports Museum

Western Pennsylvania has an unmatched sports legacy. Captured in the Museum are numerous Super Bowl, World Series, Stanley Cup and Collegiate National Championship victories, as well as the incredible high school football tradition. The Museum boasts over 100 hand-on interactive exhibits and audio-visual programs in 20,000 square feet of exhibit space. Also featured is Pittsburgh's leading role in baseball's Negro League.

The Museum is located in Pittsburgh's Strip District, just minutes from Downtown.
- 1212 Smallman St.
  Pittsburgh, PA 15222
- 412-454-6000

## SportsWorks at the Carnegie Science Center

SportsWorks is an interactive facility that combines science and sports. Thirty exhibits in all, including a 24-foot Rock Wall, You-Yo, and the Physics of Sports.
- One Allegheny Ave.
  Pittsburgh, PA 15212-5850
- (412) 237-3400

## Roberto Clemente Museum

The Roberto Clemente Museum is a museum honoring Roberto Clemente - the Major League Baseball right fielder of the Pittsburgh Pirates and Hall of Famer. The Museum features thousands of items of Clemente memorabilia, including professional sports photography, Clemente family snapshots, old uniforms, gloves, balls, bats, and seats from Forbes Field.

The Museum is located in Pittsburgh's Lawrenceville neighborhood.
- 3339 Penn Avenue
  Pittsburgh, PA 15201
- 412-621-1268

## Pittsburgh Miniature Railroad & Village

In existence since 1920, the Miniature Railroad and Village is 83 feet long by 30 feet wide and features Lionel trains. The display contains hundreds of historical and realistic scenes that depict life from the 1880s through the 1930s. The display includes over 100 animations.

The Miniature Railroad & Village is located inside the Carnegie Science Center on Pittsburgh's North Shore.
* One Allegheny Ave.
  Pittsburgh, PA 15212-5850
* (412) 237-3400

## Western Pennsylvania Model Railroad Museum

"A reality in miniature." Journey from Pittsburgh to Cumberland, Maryland on an authentically recreated route...in miniature. The museum is located in Pittsburgh's northern suburbs.
* 5507 Lakeside Drive
  Gibsonia, PA 15044

## Bicycle Heaven

Visit the worlds' largest bicycle museum and shop, which has received rave reviews from the New York Times, The Associated Press and Trip Advisor. See bikes that have been used in movies and theme bikes. All told, there are 4,000 bikes in the North Shore museum.
* 1800 Preble & Columbus Avenues
  Pittsburgh, PA 15233
* 412-734-4034

## Pittsburgh Glass Center

On a national basis, Pittsburgh has always been one of leaders in glass-making and the Glass Center is one of the top glass facilities in the United States. Tour the history and the art just east of the city.
* 5472 Penn Avenue

Pittsburgh, PA 15296
- 412-365-2145

## Future Museums

### Theatre Historical Society of America

Pittsburgh will be the home of the Theatre Historical Society of America, which moved to the city in 2017 from Chicago. Pittsburgh was chosen over 38 cities for the museum, which is the archive of the nation's largest research and preservation resources for items pertaining to movie theaters and their social and historical significance. See why Pittsburgh is the *Hollywood of the East* in later chapters.

### Brewing and Distilling Museums

Plans are underway to open two national museums to showcase the country's history in regards to brewing and distilling. Both museums are expected to open near Downtown Pittsburgh.

- **Brew: The Museum of Beer**

Expected to draw more than 400,000 visitors per year, the museum will incorporate state-of-the-art technology and interactive exhibits to tell the 10,000-year-old international story of beer. The planned 50,000 square foot facility will also show Pittsburgh's 250-year-old history of beer making.

- **Whiskey of America Museum**

Pittsburgh is the birthplace of rye whiskey and home of the famous Whiskey Rebellion. The museum will feature the history, science, culture and production of American whiskey.

**For more information on these attractions and others, please visit: visitpittsburgh.com**

# ENTERTAINMENT SPOTS

### Rivers Casino

One of Pittsburgh's premier entertainment destinations, Rivers Casino is rated as the best Overall Gaming resort in Pennsylvania. The large casino floor includes 100 table games, 3,000 slots, Poker Room, High-Roller Room, buffet and five restaurants, four bars/lounges, entertainment, free parking and a hotel.

The Casino is located on Pittsburgh's North Shore.
- 777 Casino Drive
  Pittsburgh, PA 15212
- 412-231-7777

### Station Square

Station Square is one of Pittsburgh's premier dining and entertainment destinations. The refurbished railroad station is where you can find Hard Rock Café, Grand Concourse and Rascal Flats Restaurant, as well as six other restaurants. Be sure to see the state-of-the-art Fountain at Bessemer Court, which has "Waltzing Waters Liquid Fireworks Show" of hundreds of multi-colored water jets all choreographed to music and reaching 40 feet in the air. Visit the The Freight House Shops, which houses over 20 unique retailers and a great place to discover "Pittsburgh souvenirs and novelties from around the world including toys, fashions, jewelry and cigars."
- 125 West Station Square (Southside)
  Pittsburgh, PA 15219
- 800-859-8959

### SouthSide Works

SouthSide Works is an open-air retail and entertainment life-style center located on the South Side of the city of Pittsburgh. The center includes a movie theater, numerous restaurants (including

Cheesecake Factory) and retail establishments, all within a short walk of Pittsburgh's bustling and historic South Side.

- 425 Cinema Drive
  Pittsburgh, PA 15203
- 412-381-1681

## The Waterfront Town Center

The Waterfront is an upscale, open-air, village-style shopping/ entertainment district situated along the Monongahela River. It is home to a vibrant collection of stores, restaurants, hotels and entertainment. This is where you can find the Improv Comedy Club, a dueling piano bar, an incredible AMC Loews Movie Theater and even a Dave & Buster's restaurant. More than 70 retailers and restaurants dot the village-style complex. Sandcastle Waterpark is adjacent to the Waterfront.

The shopping center is located in the Homestead area of Pittsburgh.

- 149 W. Bridge Street
  Homestead, PA 15120
- 412-476-9157

## Main Event Entertainment

A 65,000-foot entertainment complex, which includes a nightclub, restaurant, bowling alley and a broad range of entertainment options.

- 200 Quinn Drive
  Pittsburgh, PA 15275
- North Fayette Shopping District (Near the Airport)

## Future Entertainment Locations

## Kaufmann's Grand at Fifth Avenue

Located in Downtown Pittsburgh, this new complex will incorporate entertainment, retail, restaurants, a hotel and apartments. Entertainment plans include a movie theater, bowling alley, arcades and other entertainment options right in Downtown Pittsburgh.

- 400 Fifth Avenue
  Pittsburgh, PA 15219
- Downtown

Plans are underway to open two national museums to showcase the country's history in regards to brewing and distilling. Brew: The Museum of Beer is expected to draw in excess of 400,000 visitors per year. Both museums are expected to open near Downtown Pittsburgh and cater to the adult crowd – see previous pages for more information.

- **Brew: The Museum of Beer**
- **Whiskey of America Museum**

# ENTERTAINMENT VENUES

### Heinz Hall

Heinz Hall for the Performing Arts is a performing arts center and concert hall in Pittsburgh's Cultural District. Home to the Pittsburgh Symphony Orchestra (PSO) and the Pittsburgh Youth Symphony Orchestra, the 2,676-seat hall presents about 200 performances each year.

Heinz Hall is located in Downtown Pittsburgh (Cultural District).

- 600 Penn Avenue
  Pittsburgh, PA 15222
- 412-392-4900

### Benedum Center

The Benedum Center for the Performing Arts, is a primary destination in Pittsburgh's Cultural District. The 2,800-seat theater is home to Broadway shows, the Pittsburgh Opera, Pittsburgh Civic Light Opera, Pittsburgh Ballet Theatre, Pittsburgh Dance Council and Pittsburgh International Children's Theater.

The Benedum Center is located in Downtown Pittsburgh (Cultural District).

- 237 7<sup>th</sup> Street
  Pittsburgh, PA 15222
- 412-456-6666

## Byham Theater

The Byham Theater is home to a wide variety of performing arts, including dance, music, theater, film, and family-friendly events held throughout the year. 1,300 seats fill the venue.

The Byham is located in Downtown Pittsburgh (Cultural District).
- 101 6<sup>th</sup> Street
  Pittsburgh, PA 15222
- 412-456-6666

## Cabaret at Theater Square

In the heart of the Cultural District, the Cabaret is home to theatrical productions, musical productions, live music, late-night entertainment and dining. The 260-seat venue also incorporates a Backstage Bar.

The Cabaret is located in Downtown Pittsburgh (Cultural District).
- 655 Penn Avenue
  Pittsburgh, PA 15222
- 412-325-6769

## Harris Theater

The 194-seat Harris Theater is one of the most active arts facilities in the region showing art films programmed by Pittsburgh Filmmakers. The theater also hosts performances.

The theater is located in Downtown Pittsburgh (Cultural District).
- 809 Liberty Avenue
  Pittsburgh, PA 15222
- 412-681-5449

## O'Reilly Theater

The O'Reilly provides additional venues for theater, music and other performances and is the only Downtown venue to incorporate a thrust stage (surrounded by the audience on three sides). The theater features 650 seats and state-of-the-art theater technology.

The theater is located in Downtown Pittsburgh (Cultural District).
- 621 Penn Avenue
  Pittsburgh, PA 15222
- 412-316-1600

## August Wilson Center

The African American Cultural Center includes a 492-seat theater, exhibition galleries, education center and space for community events in a modernistic venue. The Cultural center, named for the famed playwright, offers African-American focused arts and events.

The Center is located in Downtown Pittsburgh (Cultural District).
- 980 Liberty Avenue
  Pittsburgh, PA 15222
- 412-471-6070

## Pittsburgh Playhouse

The Playhouse boasts 18 major productions and 235 performances per year. In 2018, a new Playhouse will open in Downtown Pittsburgh and will be home to several theaters for the Conservatory Theatre Company, Conservatory Dance Company and Playhouse Jr. The Playhouse is part of Point Park University's Conservatory of Performing Arts.
- Forbes Avenue
  Pittsburgh, PA 15222
- 412-391-4100

## Arcade Comedy Theater

Arcade Comedy Theater is downtown Pittsburgh's destination for all things comedy. The theater is located in an intimate 75-seat space which hosts stand-up, improv, sketch comedy, children's shows, variety acts, classes, workshops and more.

The theater is located in Downtown Pittsburgh (Cultural District).
- 811 Liberty Avenue
  Pittsburgh, PA 15222
- 412-339-6608

## Stage AE

Stage AE (American Eagle) is an indoor concert hall with a seating capacity of 2,500 and an outdoor amphitheater for 5,500 spectators. This multi-purpose entertainment facility is a great venue for concerts and other venues.

Stage AE is located on Pittsburgh's North Shore.
- 400 North Shore Drive
  Pittsburgh, PA 15212
- 412-229-5483

## Improv Comedy Club

The Improv is a national comedy club chain that brings national acts to the city. Eat, drink and laugh.

The Improv is located in Waterfront shopping/entertainment complex in Homestead – east of the City – and near the SandCastle Water Park.
- 166 East Bridge Street
  Homestead, PA 15120
- 412-462-5233

## Key Bank Pavilion

The Pavilion is an outdoor amphitheater that hosts national music acts. With 7,100 reserved/covered seats and 16,000 lawn seats – 23,000 spectator can view concerts at the facility.

The Pavilion is located southwest of the city in Burgettstown.
- 665 Pennsylvania Route 18
  Burgettstown, PA 15021
- 724-947-7400

## David L. Lawrence Convention Center

Located in Downtown Pittsburgh, the 1,500,000-square foot facility is home to conventions, conferences and exhibitions.
- 1000 Fort Duquesne Blvd.
  Pittsburgh, PA 15222
- 412-565-6000 or pittsburghcc.com

## Kelly-Strayhorn Theater

The theater is named in honor of two of Pittsburgh's greatest performers – Actor/Dancer Gene Kelly and Composer Billy Strayhorn. The theater focuses on high-quality, original programming of cultural, artistic and educational performances of theater, dance, music and the arts. The theater is located in Pittsburgh's East End.
- 5941 Penn Avenue
  Pittsburgh, PA 15206
- 412-363-3000

## Monroeville Convention and Events Center

100,000 square feet of multi-purpose event space used for special events, trade shows, small conventions and meetings in western Pennsylvania. Located approximately 10 miles east of Pittsburgh in Allegheny County.
- 209 Mall Boulevard

Monroeville, PA 15146
- 412-373-7300

# SPORTS ENTERTAINMENT VENUES

### Heinz Field

Home to the National Football League's Pittsburgh Steelers (and the Atlantic Coast Conference's (ACC) University of Pittsburgh Panthers), Heinz field boasts over 68,000 seats and incredible tribute to the six-time Super Bowl Champion Steelers and the nine NCAA Championships of the Panthers in the - *Great Hall*. Large concerts are also held at this facility.

Heinz Field is located on Pittsburgh's North Shore.
- 100 Art Rooney Avenue
  Pittsburgh, PA 15212
- 412-697-7700

### PNC Park

Home of Major League Baseball's Pittsburgh Pirates, PNC Park is the most beautiful stadium in all of baseball...and everyone from ESPN on down agrees. This 38,362-seat facility of the five-time World Series Champion Pirates has stunning city panoramic views, combined with excellent seat viewing and great food. A must see. Concerts are also held at this facility.

PNC Park is located on Pittsburgh's North Shore.
- 115 Federal Street
  Pittsburgh, PA 15212
- 412-321-2827

## PPG Paints Arena

Home of the National Hockey League's four-time Stanley Cup Champion Pittsburgh Penguins, this 20,000-seat facility has great seat viewing for all events held at the facility. The PPG hosts many different events as a multi-purpose facility, from concerts to the NCAA's Frozen Four Hockey National Championship.

The Arena is located in Downtown Pittsburgh.
- 1001 Fifth Avenue
  Pittsburgh, PA 15219
- 412-642-1800

## Highmark Stadium

Home of the United Soccer League's Pittsburgh Riverhounds, this multi-purpose - almost 4,000 seat facility - has great city views and plans for expansion.

Highmark Stadium is located in Station Square on Pittsburgh's Southside.
- 510 West Station Square Drive
  Pittsburgh, PA 15219
- 412-224-4900

## Petersen Events Center

Home of the Atlantic Coast Conference's University of Pittsburgh Panther's basketball team, this 12,500 seat multi-purpose arena is a great facility for viewing any event – including concerts.

The "Pete" is located on the campus of the University of Pittsburgh in the Oakland section of the city.
- 3719 Terrace Street
  Pittsburgh, PA 15261
- 412-648-3054

Other Pittsburgh Event Venues
- **Joe Walton Stadium** – Campus of Robert Morris University – 3,000 Seats
- **Arthur J, Rooney Stadium** – Campus of Duquesne University – 2,200 Seats
- **UPMC Events Center** – Campus of Robert Morris University – 4,000 Seats
- **A.J. Palombo Center** – Campus of Duquesne University – 4,400 Seats

# SPORTS ENTERTAINMENT

### Pittsburgh Steelers (National Football League)

One of the NFL's most storied franchises and six-time Super Bowl Champions (most in the NFL). The Steelers play at Heinz Field.

### Pittsburgh Pirates (Major League Baseball)

The Pirates are the second oldest franchise in MLB and five-time World Series Champions. The Pirates play at PNC Park.

### Pittsburgh Penguins (National Hockey League)

One of the NHL's strongest franchises, the Penguins are four-time Stanley Cup Champions. The Penguins play at PPG Arena

### University of Pittsburgh Panthers (National Collegiate Athletic Association – Atlantic Coast Conference

The Pitt Panthers are an integral member of the Atlantic Coast Conference (ACC) in football, basketball and other sports. The University of Pittsburgh Panthers are nine-time National Champions in football – the seventh most championships in NCAA history. The Panthers play football at Heinz Field and basketball at the Petersen Events Center, as well as other on-campus sports complexes.

## Pittsburgh Riverhounds (United Soccer League)

One of Pittsburgh's newer professional franchises, the Riverhounds play in the USL and has affiliate partnerships with Major League Soccer (MLS) franchises with its sights set on joining the MLS in the future. The Riverhounds play in Highmark Stadium.

## Pittsburgh Passion (Women's Football Alliance)

The Passion are the most storied franchise in professional women's football having won three championships and completing several undefeated seasons.

## Robert Morris University

The Colonials play Division 1-A basketball and hockey and Football Championship Series (Division 1-AA) football. The Colonials play at Joe Walton Stadium, the UPMC Events Center and the Island Sports Center.

## Duquesne University

The Dukes play Division 1-A basketball and Football Championship Series (Division 1-AA) football. The Dukes play at Rooney Field and the Palumbo Center.

# Chapter 6

# EAT/DRINK PITTSBURGH

## BEER-WINE-WHISKEY COUNTRY

**The Pittsburgh Wineries -** Please visit the respective websites for more information.

The Pittsburgh region has become home to several great wineries. According to the Pennsylvania Winery Association, Pennsylvania is a moderate "sweet spot" climate for grape cultivation and has 14,000 acres of vineyards and ranks fourth nationally in grapes grown. The abundance of vineyards has resulted in a significant increase in wine production in the State, which has seen the number of wineries grow from 27 to 123 in the past 30 years, making Pennsylvania the seventh largest producer of wines in the United States. Pennsylvania's native grapes include Concord, Catawba and Niagara, but the State also grows hybrid varieties, such as Vidal Blanc and Chambourcin, as well as the European varieties of Riesling, Chardonnay and various Cabernets'.

The next time that you partake in an excellent glass of red or white wine, look closely, it may have been made in the rolling terrain and countryside of western Pennsylvania.

- **La Casa Narcisi Winery** – Gibsonia (North Hills) – This is the largest winery in the county, which produces 20,000 gallons of high quality wine. The winery also has a restaurant with indoor and outdoor seating and a gift shop.

- **Kavic Winery** – Carnegie (Near the Airport) – A boutique winery with handcrafted, award-winning wines.
- **Carlo's Garage Winery** – Strip District (Pittsburgh) – Pittsburgh's first urban winery. Located in Enrico Biscotti Café in the heart of Pittsburgh's bustling Strip District.
- **Arsenal Cider House and Wine Cellar** – Pittsburgh (Lawrenceville) – Civil War-themed winery, which specializes in fruit wines, hard apple cider and mead (fermented honey beverage).
- **Engine House 25 Wines** – Pittsburgh (Lawrenceville) - Located in a renovated firehouse.
- **Pittsburgh Winery** – Pittsburgh (Strip District) – Boutique urban winery located in Pittsburgh's Strip District.
- **Apis Mead and Winery** – Carnegie (Near the Airport) – Winery that specializes in mead, a fermented honey beverage.
- **Bridges Wine Company** – Point Breeze (East End) – Wine Tasting and purchase wines.
- **R Wine Cellar** – Distinctive hand-crafted wines. (Strip District)

All of the wineries offer wine tasting, in various forms, and also the purchase of their product. Please visit their websites for details.

Pennsylvania has 12 wine trails that lead you to specific wineries in parts of the State. The Pittsburgh area is located on/near the Southwest Passage Wine Trail, which includes 20 or more wineries in southwestern Pennsylvania. For more information visit: www. pennsylvaniawine.com

## BREWERIES/MICROBREWS

Pittsburgh has an incredible history in the brewing industry, being the birthplace of pull-top beer cans and aluminum beer bottles to being ranked as the "#1 City for Beer Lovers" in 2016 by The Beer Institute and as one of the "Top 10 Beer Cities" by InfoGroup. Currently, there are 30 breweries in Allegheny County and 80 in western Pennsylvania. Plans are underway to open a large museum in Pittsburgh to showcase the nation's brewing history. Brew: The Museum of Beer is expected to attract over 400,000 visitors per year. Below are some of the local brewing companies creating this great history.

**Pittsburgh Brewing Company** – Known as Iron City Brewing, they are the makers of IC Light and Iron City Beers, as well as several others. (Pittsburgh/Latrobe)

**Pennsylvania Brewing Company** – Known for its authentic German brewing, they are the makers of Penn Pilsner and numerous other labels. (Pittsburgh)

**Duquesne Bottling Company** – Revitalized brewer and the maker of its signature Duquesne Beer. (Pittsburgh)

**Blockhouse Brewing** – The micro-brewing spin-off of Pittsburgh Brewing. (Pittsburgh/Latrobe)

## Other Well-Known Micro-breweries:

Brew Gentleman (Braddock)          Roundabout Brewing (Pittsburgh)

Church Brew Works (Pittsburgh)     Full Pint Wild Side (Pittsburgh)

East End Brewing (Pittsburgh)      Copper Kettle Brewing (Pittsburgh)

Full Pint Brewing (North Versailles)  Spoonwood Brewing (Pittsburgh)

Grist House Brewing (Millvale)     Rivertowne Brewing (Monroeville)

Helltown Brewing (Mount Pleasant)  Hofbrahaus (Pittsburgh)

Hitchhiker Brewing (Mt. Lebanon)   Rock Bottom Brewing (Homestead)

Hop Farm Brewing (Pittsburgh)      Milkman Brewing (Strip District)

Cobblehaus Brewing (Coraopolis)

**This is a partial list - Please visit the respective websites for more information.**

## DISTILLERS

The history of distilling in the United States is rooted in the Pittsburgh area. Pittsburgh is home to the original Rye Whiskey industry and where the historically famous Whiskey Rebellion took place. It's also where the Speakeasy was invented and has its share of Prohibition history. This history will be showcased in the future opening of the Whiskey of America Museum in Pittsburgh. Some of Pittsburgh's distillers still making history are:

**Wigle Whiskey** – Pure and traditional Pennsylvania whiskey maker. (Strip District)

**Maggie's Farm Rum Distillery** – Award winning rum distiller. (Strip District)

**Port of Pittsburgh Distillery** – Makers of rare and premium liquors from around the world. (Strip District)

**Pennsylvania Pure Distillery** – Makers of Boyd & Blair vodka. (Shaler)

**Clique Vodka** – Pittsburgh-based distributer of Latvian vodka. (Strip District)

**Stay Tuned Distillery** – Small batch craft distiller of gin. (Munhall)

**Please visit the respective websites for more information.**

## WELL-KNOWN RESTAURANTS

Pittsburgh has been named the "No. 1 Food City the U.S." by Zagat, a "Top 10 Foodie City" by Liveability.com and ranked in "Top Cities for Foodies" by NerdWallet.com. Here are some notable restaurants to visit (see the link below for the best the city has to offer):

**Lidia's Pittsburgh** – Owned by *Lidia's Italy* host and renowned chef Lidia Bastianich – Strip District

**Bar Symon** – Owned by *The Chew* host and chef, Michael Symon – Pittsburgh International Airport

**Bettis Grille 36** – Owned by Jerome Bettis (Pittsburgh Steelers) – North Shore

**Table 86** – Owned by Hines Ward (Pittsburgh Steelers) – Cranberry Township (North Hills)

**Ditka's** – Owned by famous NFL coach Mike Ditka (Pittsburgh native and University of Pittsburgh star) – Robinson Township (near the airport) and North Hills

**Anthony's Coal-Fired Pizza** – Owned by famous NFL quarterback Dan Marino (Pittsburgh native and University of Pittsburgh star) – Robinson Township and other locations

**Grand Concourse** – Located in the beautifully restored Pittsburgh & Lake Erie Railroad Station, this award-winning restaurant will provide you with a great menu and a great view – Station Square (Southside)

**LeMont** – A Five-Star restaurant with the most incredible view of the city – Mt. Washington

**Hyholde** – Rated as one of the 21 Legendary Restaurants by *Gourmet Magazine*. Dine in elegance and enjoy American inspired meals – Moon Township (Airport Area)

**Primanti's** – Pittsburgh's famous French fries on a sandwich restaurant. Strip District and other locations

**Bill's Bar & Burgers** – A New York City restaurant serving some of the nation's best burgers in the Burgh. Westin Convention Center Hotel – Downtown

**Hard Rock Café –** The famous chain rocks the Burgh. Station Square – Southside.

**For all of the best restaurants that the city has to offer visit: visitpittsburgh.com/restaurants-culinary**

Chapter 7

# NEAR-BY ENTERTAINMENT

## NEAR-BY ENTERTAINMENT
## (SHORT DRIVES FROM PITTSBURGH)

### Fallingwater

Fallingwater historic landmark, also known as the Kaufmann Residence, is a famous house designed by architect Frank Lloyd Wright in 1935. Fallingwater is located in southwestern Pennsylvania, 43 miles from Pittsburgh.

Fallingwater is located southeast of Pittsburgh.
- 1491 Mill Run Road
  Mill Run, PA 15464
- 724-329-8501

### Kentuck Knob

Kentuck Knob is another Frank Lloyd Wright designed house built in 1956. It was one of the last Wright-designed homes.

The historic landmark is located southeast of Pittsburgh.
- 723 Kentuck Road
  Dunbar, PA 15431
- 724-329-1901

## Duncan House

Duncan House is a Frank Lloyd Wright home built in 1957. Tour and stay the night just east of Pittsburgh.
- 187 Evergreen Lane
  Acme, PA 15610
- 877-833-7829

## Meadows Race Track & Casino

Harness race track and casino, located south of Pittsburgh.
- 210 Racetrack Road
  Washington, PA 15301
- 724-503-1200

## Idlewilde & Soakzone

Family-oriented amusement park with seven themed areas. Voted Best Park for Families.

The amusement park is located east of Pittsburgh.
- 2574 Route 30
  Ligonier, PA 15658
- 724-238-3666

## Meadowcroft Rock Shelter and Village

A National Historic Landmark and archaeological site, the Meadowcroft site artifacts show that the area may have been continually inhabited for more than 19,000 years, since the Paleo-Indian era. The remarkably complete archaeological site shows the earliest known evidence of human presence and the longest sequence of continuous human occupation in the New World.

The site also includes the Meadowcroft Historic Village, which is a recreated village depicting rural life in the 19th century, a Prehistoric

Indian Village, which depicts a Monongahela Indian village from 400 years ago, a Frontier Trading Post and a Trail to Trains exhibit.

Meadowcroft is operated by the Heinz History Center and is locate 27 miles south of Pittsburgh in Avella, PA.
- 401 Meadowcroft Road
  Avella, PA 15312
- 724-587-3412

## Old Economy Village

Old Economy Village is a historic settlement near Pittsburgh and administered by the Pennsylvania Historical and Museum Commission. The preserved village lies on the banks of the Ohio River. The Village is the last of three settlements established by the Harmony Society in the United States (another in Pennsylvania and one in Indiana). Established in 1824, it was designated a National Historic Landmark District in 1966 under the name of "Old Economy."

Old Economy Village is located west of Pittsburgh in the town of Ambridge.
- 270 16th Street
  Ambridge, PA 15003
- 724-266-4500

## Jimmy Stewart Museum

Museum dedicated to the local film legend of the golden age of cinema. The museum is located east of Pittsburgh
- 835 Philadelphia Street
  Indiana, PA 15701
- 800-835-4669

## Pennsylvania Trolley Museum

A museum dedicated to trolleys and includes several restored examples. The museum is located south of Pittsburgh

- 1 Museum Road
  Washington, PA 15301
- 724-228-9256

## Laurel Caverns

Laurel Caverns, formerly known as Dulaney's Cave and Laurel Hill Cave, is the largest cave in Pennsylvania. Located in Farmington, Pennsylvania; it sits on Chestnut Ridge near Uniontown, about 50 miles southeast of Pittsburgh. Tours are available of this natural wonder.
- Hopwood, PA 15445
- 724-438-2070

## Fort Necessity National Battlefield

French and Indian War - Fort Necessity National Battlefield is a National Battlefield Site in Fayette County, Pennsylvania, United States, which preserves the site of the Battle of Fort Necessity. The site is located east of Pittsburgh
- Farmington, PA 15437
- 724-329-5512

## Bushy Run Battlefield

French and Indian War - The 213 acres of forested and grassy areas that comprise Bushy Run Battlefield, Westmoreland County, Pennsylvania, can be viewed as one large historical entity. The events that transpired here in August 1763, during Pontiac's War, forever set Bushy Run apart as a place of historical significance. The battle near Bushy Run and the events of Pontiac's War leading to the battle add to the understanding of the Indian-European culture clash, which is an important theme in American history. The site is located east of Pittsburgh
- 1253 Bushy Run Road
  Jeannette, PA 15644
- 724-527-5584

## Fort Ligonier

Reconstruction of the British Fort with a museum featuring French & Indian War and Seven ears' War exhibits. The site is located east of Pittsburgh
- 200 South Market Street
  Ligonier, PA 15658
- 724-238-9701

## Westmoreland Museum of American Art

18th to 20th century American art. The museum is located east of Pittsbugh.
- 221 North Main Street
  Greensburg, PA 15601
- 724-837-1500

## Wagman Observatory

Operated by the Amateur Astronomers Association of Pittsburgh, the Nicholas E. Wagman Observatory is the first amateur astronomical observatory in western Pennsylvania dedicated to public education and enjoyment of the science of astronomy. The facility is used for recreational and scientific observations.
- 225 Kurn Road
  Tarentum, PA 15084
- 724-224-2510

## Mingo Observatory

The Mingo Creek Park Observatory is owned and operated by the Amateur Astronomers Association of Pittsburgh and is dedicated to public education and enjoyment of the science of astronomy. The facility is used for recreational and scientific observations.
- 1 Shelter 10 Road
  Finleyville, PA 15332
- 724-348-6150

# Chapter 8

# THE PARKS OF PITTSBURGH

Pittsburgh has close to 200 green building projects and is well-known as one of the "greenest" cities in the country with an abundance of outdoor activities in lush surroundings.

## ALLEGHENY COUNTY PARKS

### North Park

Allegheny County park that features 3,075 acres – 65 acre lake for kayaking and fishing, golf course, pool, ice rink, ball fields, nature center, trails and shelters.

North Park is located north of Pittsburgh in the suburbs of McCandless, Pine and Hampton.
- Pearce Mill Road
  Allison Park, PA 15101
- 724-935-1766

### South Park

Allegheny County park that features 2,013 acres – Game preserve featuring a herd of American buffalo, golf courses, wave pool, ice rink, skate park, ball fields, trails, nature center and shelters.

South Park is located south of Pittsburgh in the suburbs of Bethel Park and South Park.

- Buffalo Drive
  South Park, PA 15129
- 412-835-4810

## Boyce Park

Allegheny County park that features 1,096 acres - wave pool, downhill skiing, snow tubing, skate park, ball fields, archery range, tails, nature center and shelters.

Boyce Park is located east of Pittsburgh in the suburbs of Monroeville and Plum.

- 675 Old Frankstown Road
  Pittsburgh, PA 15239
- 724-327-0338

## Settlers Cabin Park

Allegheny County park that features 1,610 acres – wave pool, dive pool, historic log cabin, trails, tennis courts and shelters. The Pittsburgh Botanic Gardens is adjacent to the park.

Settlers Cabin park is located west of Pittsburgh in the suburbs of Robinson and North Fayette.

- 1225 Greer Road
  Oakdale, PA 15071
- 412-787-2750

## Hartwood Acres

Allegheny County park that features 629 acres – historic mansion, cross-country skiing, trails.

The park is located north of Pittsburgh in the suburbs of Hampton and Indiana.

- 200 Hartwood Acres
  Pittsburgh, PA 15238
- 412-767-9200

## Deer Lakes Park

Allegheny County park that features 1,180 acres – fishing lakes, observatory, multi-purpose fields, trails and shelters.

The park is located northeast of Pittsburgh in Tarentum.
- 1090 Baileys Run Road
  Tarentum, PA 15084
- 724-265-3520

## Harrison Hills Park

Allegheny County park that features 500 acres – ponds, birding area, trails, scenic overlook, environmental learning center, soccer fields and shelters.

The park is located north of the city in the suburb of Harrison.
- 5200 Freeport Road
  Natrona Heights, PA 15065
- 724-295-3570

## White Oak Park

Allegheny County park that features 810 acres – trails, multi-purpose fields, wedding garden, volley ball, bocce, horseshoes and shelters.

The park is located south of the city in the suburb of White Oak.
- 3 Muse Lane
  White Oak, PA 15131
- 412-678-3773

# CITY OF PITTSBURGH PARKS

### Schenley Park

The park boasts 456 acres, golf course, swimming pool, sports complex, lake and is a haven for outdoor enthusiast. The Phipps Conservatory is located in the park.

The park is located east of Downtown in the Oakland section of the city.

### Frick Park

The park boasts over 250 acres, lawn bowling, tennis courts, athletic fields, environmental center, large playground and bird viewing area.

The park is located east of the city near the Squirrel Hill neighborhood.

### Highland Park

The park boasts a bike track, swimming pool, volleyball courts and walking and jogging trails. The park is adjacent to the Pittsburgh Zoo and Aquarium.

Highland Park is located east of Downtown in the Highland Park neighborhood.

### Riverview Park

The park boasts extensive trails, pool, athletic fields, playgrounds and shelters. The Allegheny Observatory is located in the park.

Riverview Park is located north of Downtown near the North Shore.

# LOCAL STATE PARKS

### Point State Park

This historic park is located in Downtown Pittsburgh at the confluence of the three rivers. Used primarily for large city events, the park also has walking and jogging trails and boasts the large fountain that churns 20,000 gallons of water a minute, which has become a symbol of Pittsburgh. This is the only State park in the country in the middle of a city. The Fort Pitt Museum and Fort Pitt Blockhouse are located in the park.

The park is located in Downtown Pittsburgh on the western edge.

### Moraine State Park

The park boasts 16,725-acres, as well as hiking/biking/walking trails, large lake used for swimming (with beach), boating and fishing. Camping is also available, as are a number of winter-related activities.

The park is located north of the city in Butler County.

### Raccoon Creek State Park

The park boasts 7,572 acres and a 100-acre lake used for swimming, boating and fishing, trails and camp grounds.

The park is located west of the city in Beaver County.

### McConnell's Mill State Park

The park boasts 2,546 acres with hiking, boating, fishing and the iconic gristmill.

The park is located north of the city Lawrence County.

## Ohiopyle State Park

The park boasts 19,052 acres and well-known white-water rafting. Also available are trails, fishing, camping and winter activities.

The park is located east of Pittsburgh in Fayette County.

# TRAILS

Pittsburgh has 24 miles of riverfront trails, which will take you on journey to the nation's capital.

### The Great Allegheny Passage

A 335 mile, traffic free corridor located between Pittsburgh and Washington D.C. The trail is used for biking, walking and hiking. The trail also connects with smaller trails leading directly into both cities.

### Montour Trail

The Montour Trail extends the Pittsburgh-end of The Great Allegheny Passage westward towards the Pittsburgh International Airport for walking, hiking and biking. The trail has been named the *Trail of the Year* for 2017 by the Pennsylvania Department of Conservation and Natural Resources.

### Hollow Oak Land Trust

Located near the Pittsburgh International Airport, the Hollow Oak Land Trust comprises of approximately 500 acres of preservation land, which are used for hiking, biking and relaxation.

## Future Trail

### Lewis and Clark Trail

The National Parks Service is considering extending the historic Lewis and Clark trail to Pittsburgh. Pittsburgh is where the official Lewis and Clark expedition began with the construction of the 55-foot keelboat and where Merriweather Lewis departed from after the boat was completed. The trail follows the entire route and currently runs from the Pacific to the mid-west.

# Chapter 9

# GOLF AND SKI PITTSBURGH

## GOLF COURSES

The Pittsburgh area features numerous courses in a state that has the most courses per capita in the country. In 2016, according to Golf Datatech, the Pittsburgh-area golf courses had the largest increase in rounds played than any city in the country (12% increase). The area has eight courses rated "Outstanding" or "four-out-of-five Stars" by *Golf Digest*. Of course, this is also Arnold Palmer's backyard.

### Oakmont

Few courses in the world of golf have a reputation and tradition as well-respected as Oakmont. Oakmont has hosted more PGA and USGA championships than any other course in the United States: Eight U.S. Opens, two women's U.S. Opens, three PGA Championships and five U.S. Amateurs Championships. Considered by many to be the most difficult course in North America.

Oakmont is located a few miles northeast of the city in the suburb of Oakmont.

- 1233 Hulton Road
  Oakmont, PA 15139
- 412-828-8000

## Pittsburgh Field Club

The Field Club has hosted a PGA Championship, as well as a Western Open. This impressive course is located just northeast of the city.

The Club is located in the suburb of Fox Chapel.
- 121 Field Club Drive
  Pittsburgh, PA 15238
- 412-963-8500

## Quicksilver

The Quicksilver Golf Club is an award-winning course that has hosted the Senior PGA Tour, as well as the Ben Hogan Tour (Web.com Tour). It's been rated the best public course in Pittsburgh eight times, best public course in Western Pennsylvania six times and has also been rated as one of the Top 15 Courses in Pennsylvania by *Golf Week Magazine*.

Quicksilver is located west of the city near the airport – in Midway.
- 2000 Quicksilver Road
  Midway, PA 15060
- 724-796-1594

## Mystic Rock at Nemacolin

This Pete Dye-design course has been rated in both Golf Digest and Golfweek numerous times as one of the best courses in the State of Pennsylvania.

The course is located on the Nemacolin resort – southeast of the city.
- 1001 Layfayette Drive
  Farmington, PA 15437
- 866-344-6957

## Olde Stonewall

A premier public course and often rated as one of the top courses by both Golf Digest and Golf Magazine,

The course is located north of the city – approximately 40 minutes in Ellwood City,

- 1495 Mercer Road
  Ellwood City, PA 16117
- 724-752-4653

## Robert Morris University – Golf Dome

The university operates a large, two-level golf dome enabling golfers to practice their driving and iron skills, as well as their pitching and putting skills – all in a climate controlled setting. The golf dome is located in the Island Sports Center, which is just west of Pittsburgh on Neville Island.

- 7600 Grand Avenue
  Pittsburgh, PA 15225
- 412-397-3335

Pittsburgh has numerous other golf courses in the area, both 18 and 9 hole options.

**For more information on golfing in the Pittsburgh area: visitpittsburgh.com**

# SKI RESORTS

The Pittsburgh area is in the Appalachian Mountain range and skiing goes with the territory.

### Seven Springs Mountain Resort

An all-season resort, located just east of the Pittsburgh area in Seven Springs (Champion), Pennsylvania. The resort has 33 slopes and trails, 7 Terrain Parks and 10 lifts. Enjoy skiing, snowboarding and snow tubing in winter and zip lining, golfing, fishing and hiking in summer. The resort includes a hotel and restaurants.

- 777 Waterwheel Dr.

Seven Springs, PA 15622
- 800-452-2223

## Hidden Valley Resort

Hidden Valley has 26 slopes and trails, two Terrain Parks and 9 lifts for skiing and snowboarding. The resort has a hotel and restaurants and is located east of the Pittsburgh area.
- One Craighead Drive
  Hidden Valley, PA 15502
- 814-443-8000

## Laurel Mountain Ski Resort

Located in Laurel Mountain State Park, this resort boasts some of the steepest slopes and vertical drops in the state. The resort has 20 slopes and trails and 5 lifts. Lodging packages and dining are available. The resort is located east of Pittsburgh.
- 770 Ligonier Road
  Rector, PA 15677
- 724-238-2801

## Boyce Park

Part of the Allegheny County parks system and located in the eastern part of the county (just outside of Pittsburgh); Boyce has skiing, snowboarding and snow tubing. Boyce has 10 slopes and several lifts.
- 675 Old Frankstown Road
  Plum, PA 15239
- 724-327-8798

**For more information on skiing in the Pittsburgh area: visitpittsburgh.com**

## Chapter 10

# ANNUAL EVENTS AND HOLIDAY ATTRACTIONS IN PITTSBURGH

## JANUARY-FEBRUARY-MARCH

Pittsburgh Restaurant Week's Winter Celebration

Celebrate a week of Downtown festivities highlighting Pittsburgh's incredible restaurant and dining scene. Pittsburgh has been ranked as the #1 Food City by *Zagat*. (January)

Pittsburgh RV Show

RV and camping enthusiasts come from near and far to see the newest models and receive expert advice. Convention Center. – (January)

Pittsburgh's Women "Wine & Whiskey" Winterfest

Pennsylvania wineries provide unlimited one ounce tastings in an exciting, fun and pampering event. Downtown Convention Center. (January)

Pittsburgh's Wine on the Three Rivers

Sample and purchase the best of Pennsylvania wines. Downtown Convention Center (January)

## Remodeling Expo

The newest styles and materials are show cased at the Downtown Convention Center. (January)

## World of Wheels Custom Car Show

Custom car show that everyone is sure to enjoy. Downtown Convention Center. (January)

## Three Rivers Boat Show (January)

See all of the latest boats, equipment and gear for the up-coming season. Downtown Convention Center. (January)

## Tri-State Outdoor Expo (January)

The newest in outdoor gear and equipment is showcased at the Downtown Convention Center, (January)

## Pittsburgh Travel Showcase (January)

All of your travel needs and planning assistance located under one roof. Downtown Convention Center (January)

## Kidapalooza

A festival of fun for the entire family in this indoor carnival. Monroeville Convention Center. (January/February)

## Monster Jam

Monster trucks invade the PPG Paints Arena in an incredible display. (February)

## Pittsburgh International Auto Show

See all of the latest cars and trucks from around the world – all under one roof. Downtown –Convention Center. (February)

## Pittsburgh College Fair

Numerous colleges and universities are available to discuss your educational needs under one roof at the Downtown Convention Center. (February)

## Lights, Glamour, Action

Celebrate the Academy Awards and walk the Red Carpet with the Pittsburgh Film Office's gala event. Rotating Downtown Locations. (February/March)

## St. Patrick's Day Parade

The Downtown parade began in 1869 and is one of the Top 3 largest parades in the United States. Pittsburgh has been ranked as the best place to celebrate St. Patrick's Day by Niche.com. (March)

## Pittsburgh Home & Garden Show

Pittsburgh's David L. Lawrence Convention Center brings in spring in the largest home event in Pennsylvania. (March)

## Pittsburgh's WineFest "acular"

Wine tasting, food trucks and entertainment. Downtown Convention Center. (March)

## Pittsburgh Knit and Crochet/Creative Arts Festival

Knit, crochet, quilt and creative arts festival. Downtown – Convention Center. (March)

Pittsburgh Fringe Festival

Theatre festival of performance arts. (rotating locations) – (March)

**April-May-June**

Pittsburgh Craft Beer Week

Features Pittsburgh's craft beer culture. Downtown (April)

Steel City Con

Comic Con – held annually. (Monroeville) (April)

Lawrenceville's Art All Night

Free grassroots community art show. Lawrenceville – (April)

Pittsburgh Wine Festival

Taste from hundreds of wines from around the world, along with great food. Heinz Field (May)

Pittsburgh International Children's Festival

Performances from around the world, hands-on activities, scavenger hunt and much more. Cultural District. (May)

Pittsburgh Race for the Cure

Marathon-style race for charity. Schenley Park (Oakland) – (May)

Pyrofest

Fireworks festival. Butler County – Coopers Lake (May)

## Pittsburgh Health and Fitness Festival

See the latest in fitness trends and equipment. Downtown - Convention Center. (May)

## Pittsburgh Marathon

Pittsburgh's marathon. Downtown (May)

## Soldiers & Sailors Memorial Hall & Museum Memorial Day Celebration

Celebrating Memorial Day at Pittsburgh's war history museum. Oakland - (May)

## Anthrocon

The "Furry" convention. Animal costume-themed gathering. (June)

## Three Rivers Arts Festival

Pittsburgh's largest art and craft festival. (Downtown) – (June)

## Pittsburgh PrideFest and Pride in the Street

Equality festival and parade. Downtown – (June)

## Pittsburgh Jazz Live International Festival

Pittsburgh's jazz festival. Downtown - (June)

## July-August-September

## Pittsburgh 4th of July Celebration

Pittsburgh's incredible fireworks display and music celebrates the 4th of July. Point State Park – (July)

## Pittsburgh Vintage Grand Prix

Vintage race cars roar back to life in this annual race event. Schenley Park – (July)

## PicklesBURGH

A pickle festival held on the Rachel Carson Bridge. Downtown – (July)

## BikeFest

A festival celebrating all-things-bicycling. Downtown – (August)

## Pittsburgh Restaurant Week's Summer Celebration

Celebrate Pittsburgh's fantastic restaurants across the city. (August)

## Bloomfield Little Italy Days

Pittsburgh's biggest Italian festival. Bloomfield section of Pittsburgh – (August)

## Pittsburgh Renaissance Festival

Return to the days of 16th century festivals. West Newton (August/ September)

## Pittsburgh Three Rivers Regatta

Pittsburgh celebrates its rivers with its annual regatta. Downtown – (August)

## Pittsburgh Triathlon

Pittsburgh's triathlon. Point State Park (Downtown) – (August)

Pedal Pittsburgh

Over 3,000 bikes take to Pittsburgh's trails. (August)

Pittsburgh Comedy Festival

A four-day celebration of all things funny. Oakland – (August)

Thrival Innovation & Music Festival

Multiple day event of innovation and music. City Locations. (August)

The Kickoff and Rib Festival

Pittsburgh's rib festival is combined with the opening of the college football season. Heinz Field – (September)

Pittsburgh Folk Festival

Take part in Pittsburgh's diverse cultures with entertainment and food. Oakland (September)

Fair in the Park

Annual contemporary fine art and craft festival. (Mellon Park) (September)

Pittsburgh Labor Day Parade

Pittsburgh celebrates its labor history with a grand parade. Downtown – (September)

Penn Brewery Oktoberfest

Pittsburgh's authentic German brewery throws the ultimate fest. North Shore/North Side (September)

Pittsburgh Pierogi Fest

Celebration of Pittsburgh's comfort food. Kennywood Park (September)

Pittsburgh Comic Con

Large comic book and pop-culture convention. Convention Center – (September)

Pittsburgh Cocktail Week

Celebrate libations of all sorts during various weeks and locations. (September/December)

Pittsburgh Irish Festival

Celebrate Pittsburgh's Irish heritage. West Homestead/ Riverplex – (September)

Penn's Colony Festival

Pittsburgh's regional celebration of the French & Indian War era. Saxonburg (September)

Pittsburgh Fashion Week

View the top trending fashions from close to 30 designers. Southside (September)

Richard S. Caliguiri City of Pittsburgh Great Race

10K race (and a 5K) that winds through the city to Downtown. Frick Park (September)

## October-November-December

### Pittsburgh Columbus Day Parade

Pittsburgh celebrates the official discovery of America with a gala parade. Downtown – (October)

### The ScareHouse

One of America's top haunted houses. Etna – (October)

### Kennywood Phantom Fright Nights

Celebrate the Halloween season at Pittsburgh's famous amusement park. West Mifflin – (October)

### Pittsburgh ZooBoo

Celebrate the Halloween season at the Pittsburgh Zoo. Highland Park – (October)

### Head of the Ohio Boat Race

2.8-mile Crew race on the Allegheny River. Downtown – (October)

### VIA Music Festival

A music festival for the city. Multiple locations in the city – (October)

### Celebrate the Season Parade

Pittsburgh officially begins the holiday season with a big parade. Downtown – (November)

### EQT Ten Miler

10-mile race through the city. Station Square – (November)

## Three Rivers Film Festival

Independent cinema is celebrated via films and filmmakers from around the world. Various – (November)

## Light Up Night

Pittsburgh kicks-off the holiday season as the city "lights-up" in grand style. Downtown – (November)

## Pittsburgh Holiday Market

A traditional German-style Christmas market for all of your holiday needs. Downtown – (December)

## Kennywood Holiday Lights

Celebrate the holiday season at Pittsburgh's famous amusement park. West Mifflin – (December)

## Piratefest

The thoughts of baseball break the winter with this annual Pittsburgh Pirates festival. Convention Center – (Downtown)

## First Night Pittsburgh

Celebrate New Year's Eve in grand style with numerous events throughout Downtown Pittsburgh. (December)

# PITTSBURGH'S HOLIDAY ATTRACTIONS

Starting at Thanksgiving and flowing into the New Year, Pittsburgh has an abundance of holiday festivities to offer.

## Light-Up Night

The annual holiday Light-Up Night Celebration is held in November and kicks-off the season. This free event features the famous Santa Claus "fireball" tree lighting, numerous tree lighting celebrations, entertainment, activities, music and fireworks throughout downtown Pittsburgh. All of this as the city lights shine for the season.

## The Holiday Market

Light-Up Night also signifies the start of Pittsburgh's Holiday Market in Market Square. Based on Germany's famous Christkindlmarkt, the holiday shopping village includes vendors from around the world. The Market includes unique gifts, cultural music and food, as well as Santa's house all in downtown Pittsburgh.

## Pittsburgh's Celebrate the Season Holiday Parade

Held in late November, the season kicks-off with bands, floats and national celebrities marching through the heart of the city. Santa, of course, brings in the season at the end.

## Santa's From Around the World

Visit this very unique display of life-size Santa's from around the world in the PPG Place Wintergarden. Each Santa is ornately displayed with related history and paintings from each country. Enjoy train and gingerbread house displays, as well as live holiday music. PPG Place is located in downtown Pittsburgh.

## The Pittsburgh Crèche

No other city in the world can boast of an authentic, life-size replica of the Vatican crèche. This one-of-a-kind replica was created by the same sculptor that made the Vatican display. The crèche is located at the USX Tower in downtown Pittsburgh.

## The Pittsburgh Unity Tree

A Pittsburgh tradition, this tree covers the entire corner of a downtown building and has signified the holidays for generations.

## Pittsburgh Ice Rink at PPG Place

Larger than the ice rink in Rockefeller Center, this downtown Pittsburgh ice rink includes a majestic Christmas tree at its center and is surrounded by PPG Place – also known as the "Ice Castle."

## The Kaufman's Holiday Windows

Once displayed at Kaufman's Department Store, these ornate, animated scenes are still are visible in downtown Pittsburgh during the holiday season – at either their original location or in other downtown buildings.

## Neapolitan Presepio

Considered one the finest Nativity scenes of its kind in the world, this Pittsburgh holiday tradition includes an entire village of highly detailed, hand crafted figures. The Presepio is located in the Carnegie Museum in Pittsburgh's Oakland section.

## Phipps Conservatory and Botanical Gardens' Winter Light Garden and Flower Show

A festive and holiday atmosphere is depicted in a wonderland of gardens. The Conservatory is located in Pittsburgh's Oakland section.

## The Pittsburgh Miniature Railroad & Village

Located on Pittsburgh's North Shore at the Carnegie Science Center, this holiday tradition has been publically displayed since 1954. In existence since 1920, the Miniature Railroad and Village is 83 feet long by 30 feet wide and features Lionel trains. The display contains hundreds of historical and realistic scenes that depict life from the 1880s through the 1930s. The display includes over 100 animations.

## Western Pennsylvania Model Railroad Museum

"A reality in miniature." Journey from Pittsburgh to Cumberland, Maryland on an authentically recreated route in miniature. The museum is located in Pittsburgh's northern suburb of Gibsonia and primarily opens during the holidays.

## Kennywood Holiday Lights

The amusement park is transformed into a holiday wonderland of one million lights and light shows, including the famous light show on the lagoon. The Gingerbread Express train travels the park and live holiday music fills the air. Kennywood is located in the Pittsburgh suburb of West Mifflin.

## Hartwood Acres

Tour the Hartwood Mansion as it is decked for the holidays, and take part in the Holiday Musical Tea and Tour. This is also the location of Pittsburgh's most popular holiday light display, which is currently not operating at this time. Other local holiday light displays are the Christmas Light-Up Celebration in Clinton, Overly's Country Christmas and Shadrack's Christmas Wonderland. Hartwood is located in Hartwood Acres Park in the northern suburb of Hampton Township. **Bottom of Form**

## First Night Pittsburgh

Ring in the New Year with First Night Pittsburgh in the downtown Cultural District. This large, family-friendly event includes 150 events at numerous locations downtown. The countdown to the New Year includes live music and arts focused events.

Chapter 11

# THE UNIVERSITIES
# OF PITTSBURGH

## IN ALLEGHENY COUNTY

### University of Pittsburgh

The University of Pittsburgh is a state-related research university – also known as Pitt – and home to approximately 30,000 students. The university specializes in medical and engineering programs, but offers a broad array of majors in many disciplines. The university is highly-acclaimed and is often rated in the Top 25 public universities and has also been rated in the Top 25 in the world in "Best higher education research institutions." It is also home to the famous Cathedral of Learning.

The university is located east of the city in the Oakland section.
*   4200 Fifth Avenue
    Pittsburgh, PA 15260
*   412-624-4141

### Carnegie Mellon University

One of the top universities in the country, CMU is highly acclaimed for its computer science, robotics, engineering and drama programs.

Carnegie Mellon is located east of the city in the Oakland section.
- 5000 Forbes Avenue
  Pittsburgh, PA 15213
- 412-268-2000

## Duquesne University

A Catholic university, Duquesne boasts ten schools/institutions and 190 academic programs for it's over 10,000 students.

Duquesne is located in Downtown Pittsburgh.
- 600 Forbes Avenue
  Pittsburgh, PA 15282
- 412-396-6000

## Robert Morris University

Robert Morris University has established a well-known reputation as a business-related university, specializing in majors such as accounting, among many others. The university boasts Schools of Business, Education, Communication, Nursing and Engineering/Mathematics/Science.

RMU is located in the western suburb of Moon Township.
- 6001 University Boulevard
  Moon Township, PA 15108
- 800-762-0097

## Point Park University

Point Park University is a liberal arts institution that offers a wide-array of majors, but is best known for Cinema Arts, Theatre Arts and Dance.

The University is located in Downtown Pittsburgh.
- 201 Wood Street
  Pittsburgh, PA 15222

- 412-391-4100

## LaRoche University

LaRoche is a private, Catholic university with a wide-array of majors located on a suburban campus.

The university is located in the northern suburbs of Pittsburgh.
- 9000 Babcock Blvd.
  Pittsburgh, PA 15237
- 412-367-9300

## Chatham University

Chatham is an urban-based university that features majors such as Architecture and Health Sciences.

The university is located in Pittsburgh's Shadyside neighborhood.
- 1 Woodland Road
  Pittsburgh, PA 15232
- 412-365-1100

## Carlow University

Carlow is a private, Catholic university located on an urban campus. It offers a number of degrees from business to nursing.

Carlow is located in the Oakland section of Pittsburgh.
- 3333 Fifth Avenue
  Pittsburgh, PA 15213
- 800-333-2275

## Community College of Allegheny College (CCAC)

CCAC has over 60,000 students and offers associates degrees at the highest level. Most credits are transferrable to four-year institutions. The college has four campuses in the county.

The main campus is located on Pittsburgh's North Shore.

- 800 Allegheny Avenue
  Pittsburgh, PA 15233
- 412-237-3100

# Chapter 12

# PITTSBURGH NEIGHBORHOODS AND SUBURBS

Pittsburgh has 90 neighborhoods for you to discover, each with its own flavor.

**Downtown**

Pittsburgh's Downtown is known as the "Golden Triangle" and it sits at the center of 90 neighborhoods. It is also one of the fastest growing neighborhoods in the city in regard to population. Downtown is no longer just the epicenter for Fortune 500 companies and commerce, it is now home for many. Numerous condominium and apartment complexes are sprouting throughout Downtown in a building boom that includes hotels, restaurants and new retail establishments. All of these amenities are within walking distance to a thriving cultural district, plazas, parks and sporting venues. Enjoy outdoor activities in Point State Park, Market Square, Mellon Square, U.S. Steel Plaza, PPG Plaza and many others. As you exit the Fort Pitt Tunnel – Downtown bursts into view and that it why Pittsburgh is said to be the "only city with an entrance."

**Bloomfield**

Bloomfield is known as Pittsburgh's "Little Italy." Italian restaurants and shops dot the main street. Bloomfield is also the location of one of the largest festivals – Little Italy Days. The Bloomfield Bridge connects the neighborhood to Oakland's universities and cultural attractions.

## East Liberty

East Liberty has been in an enormous state of revitalization, which has resulted in hotels, restaurants and the refurbishment of historic buildings. To prove it is on the right path, Google established a large presence of offices in the neighborhood.

## Lawrenceville

Pittsburgh's hippest and trendiest neighborhood, Lawrenceville is packed with restaurants and shops and is known to be home to the artistic crowd. The New York Times recently named it a "go-to" destination.

## Mount Washington

Possibly the neighborhood with the greatest view in the entire country, Mount Washington is also renowned for fine dining. Grandview Avenue provides incredible views of the city and is also the headquarters of both the Duquesne and Monongahela Inclines. Undoubtedly one of the most visited tourist areas in Pittsburgh – Mount Washington shows off one of the most beautiful skylines in the world.

## North Shore – North Side

Home to some of Pittsburgh's greatest attractions: PNC Park, Heinz Field, Rivers Casino, Andy Warhol Museum, Carnegie Science Center, Sportsworks, The National Aviary, Pittsburgh Children's Museum and the Mattress Factory (art museum). The iconic neighborhood also boasts areas such as the Mexican War Streets and is considered the best place to watch Pittsburgh's incredible fireworks displays.

## Oakland

Oakland is considered the academic, cultural and medical center of the city. This is the home of the University of Pittsburgh, Carnegie-Mellon University, The Carnegie Museum of Natural History, The Carnegie Museum of Art, Soldiers and Sailors Hall and Schenley Park. One of Pittsburgh's most international neighborhoods, you will find numerous restaurants, coffee shops and trendy shopping spots. It also boasts some incredible architecture.

## Shadyside

Shadyside is an up-scale neighborhood with tree-lined streets and Victorian homes. It is also home to one of the best neighborhood shopping districts where small boutiques, restaurants and galleries, intermingle with national retailers. Shadyside is also known for unique events and festivals.

## Southside

A National Historic District boasting Victorian architecture, Southside is also filled with restaurants, art galleries, theaters, shops and live music venues. South Side's East Carson Street has been called the "Great American Main Street." Southside is also the location of Station Square, Southside Works and Highmark Stadium.

## Squirrel Hill

Tree-lined streets and over 1,100 acres of parkland is what you notice first about the Squirrel Hill neighborhood. In between the greenery are nice residential areas and a great business district.

## Strip District

The Strip is primarily known to be Pittsburgh's international marketplace. Incredible ethnic stores and shops cover the main street, as do restaurants. The shopping district is filled with sidewalk vendors and some of the freshest foods in the city. Once known primarily for commerce, the Strip is becoming more residential with an incredible condo/apartment building boom near the main street.

### The Hill District

Located near downtown, it is home of the once famous jazz-based street of Wylie Avenue and the renowned Crawford Grill.

## THE SUBURBS

Pittsburgh has some outstanding suburbs and they are typically considered to be located in the "hills" – North Hills, South Hills, East Hills and West Hills. The hills refer to the fact that Pittsburgh sits in the foothills of the Appalachian Mountains. Below are some of significant suburbs in Allegheny County:

### North Hills

Wexford/Pine – One of the more excellent combinations of residential and rural living.

Richland/Gibsonia – Exclusive neighborhoods and tree-lined communities.

Fox Chapel – One of Pittsburgh's most exclusive suburbs

Hampton – An affluent neighborhood that is a great place for families.

Others include the tree-lined streets of Shaler Township, the exclusive hometown feel of Oakmont, the traditional hometowns of Sharpsburg and Millvale, the up-scale Bradford Woods and the bustling suburbs of McCandless, Franklin Park and Ross.

## South Hills

Mt. Lebanon – Upper scale community with boutique shops.

Upper Saint Clair – Upper scale community with a mall.

Bethel Park – Great residential community with parks.

Others include South Park, which is home to the county park with same name – not to mention its herd of buffalo, Dormont with its busy business district and Baldwin with its suburban feel.

## East Hills

Monroeville – A shopping and residential hub.

Churchhill – A traditional residential community.

Plum - Home of Boyce Park and its ski slopes.

Forrest Hills – Well-known as "A Tree City, USA."

Others include West Mifflin, which is home to Kennywood Park – America's favorite traditional park – and West Homestead, which is home to Sandcastle Water Park and The Waterfront shopping district.

## West Hills

Robinson – Great residential location with ample shopping and dining options.

Moon Twp. – One of the largest townships, Moon is known as a great residential community.

North Fayette – A bustling shopping district highlights this township.

Sewickley – One of the more exclusive suburbs with boutique shops.

Sewickley Heights – Very exclusive residential suburb.

Others include Coraopolis, with its growing business district and quaint residential streets, Findlay Township – home of the Pittsburgh International Airport and the quiet residential community of Crescent Township.

## THE PEOPLE OF PITTSBURGH

The people of Pittsburgh are often considered its greatest asset. They are as unique as they are loyal to their hometown, and not necessarily just in relation to their very successful sports franchises. They are descendants of countries from around the world and have held their traditions and values throughout the generations. A majority of the population are of European ancestry. They are descendants of eastern European countries, as well as large populations of those of Italian, Irish, Polish and German heritage.

They are hard-working and resilient, as can be seen by the fall of the steel industry and the resurgence we see today. The people of Pittsburgh are an example for many to follow in relation to transforming a city. They have their own unique dialect, yet it is often only spoken amongst themselves. One of the greatest traits many have found in Pittsburghers is their friendliness. As the old saying goes...Ask someone from Pittsburgh for directions and not only will they provide them in detail, but don't be surprised that they'll lead you there.

Chapter 13

# THINGS YOU SHOULD KNOW ABOUT PITTSBURGH

## COMPANIES (With a Large Presence in Pittsburgh)

Pittsburgh is well-known for its manufacturing history and still boasts the likes of U.S. Steel and ALCOA in that realm, but it is the city's advancement in technology, engineering, medicine, education, finance, robotics, self-driving vehicles, natural gas and the movie industry that has transformed the economy into a "Knowledge Base" and created a very bright future. Pittsburgh ranks in the Top 10 cities for corporate headquarters. The list below contains some of the largest companies in the United States, if not the world, but Pittsburgh is an attractive evolving marketplace that now includes a large presence of cutting-edge companies, such as Google, Uber, Disney, Facebook, Apple and Amazon, as well as Duolingo, Jawbone, Resumator, TrueFit, Carnegie Learning and 4Moms.

- **Google** has over 400 employees in Pittsburgh working on engineering projects, as well as Product Search, ad quality and infrastructure.
- **Uber** has headquartered its self-driving vehicle program in Pittsburgh and will invest $1 billion in the project. Uber is expected to have 1,000 local employees by 2018. Uber has made

Pittsburgh the first city in the world to test self-driving taxis and they also operate a large, state-of-the-art test track in the city.

- **Ford Motor Company** is investing $1 billion in Pittsburgh-based Argo AI to develop technology for its own self-driving vehicles. Argo AI plans to hire 200 additional employees in 2017, primarily in Pittsburgh.
- **Facebook** has opened a facility in Pittsburgh dedicated to its Oculus virtual reality division. The research facility will develop computer vision for augmented reality.
- **Disney** operates its Disney Research Lab in Pittsburgh where it works with Carnegie Mellon University to enhance Disney's robotics, computer vision, speech understanding, motion capture and machine learning aspects. The lab also performs research in radio and antennas, as well as sports visualization. The Disney Research Lab works with Walt Disney Parks and Resorts and other units of the Walt Disney Company, as well as ESPN.
- **Apple** recently secured 26,000 square feet of space in a new building in Pittsburgh for a research project. Apple has been in Pittsburgh for a number of years working with the Pittsburgh Collaborative Innovation Center.
- **Amazon** has opened a corporate office in Pittsburgh, which works with the Amazon Echo and Alexa machine translation, Amazon web services and their voice-controlled intelligent assistant. Amazon has also established local distribution centers and has hundreds of employees in the area. In addition, per CNN and Forbes, Pittsburgh is considered a leading contender for Amazon's second headquarters site.
- **Netflix** plans to establish a filming studio just north of Pittsburgh (Allegheny County) to film their television series programs.
- **Microsoft** maintains its Mid-Atlantic District office in Pittsburgh and also participates with the Pittsburgh Collaborative Innovation Center.
- **Intel** operates a research lab in Pittsburgh to accelerate the development of new computing and communications technology.

## Pittsburgh: A Leader in Robotics

Pittsburgh is a powerhouse in the robotics industry, so much so that the *Wall Street Journal* has referred to the city as "Roboburgh." As far back as 1979, Pittsburgh's Carnegie-Mellon University created the Robotics Institute, in conjunction with the Pittsburgh-based National Robotics Engineering Center, making the city a leader in robotics research and leading to advances in space exploration, national security, transportation, medicine, agriculture and mining. Pittsburgh has been the birthplace and leader in robotics-based innovations, such as autonomous vehicles, space-based units – such as the Mars Rover and industrial robots.

In 2017, the Department of Defense announced it would join with 100 companies and foundations to open the Advanced Robotics Manufacturing Innovation Hub in Pittsburgh. The nonprofit will invest $253 million into the project, which will develop autonomous manufacturing processes.

Three world leaders in robotics are based in the area - RedZone Robotics, Argo AI and Aesynt. To show the magnitude of the industry in Pittsburgh, the following cutting-edge companies are listed as also having a presence in the region: American Robot Corporation, Google PittPatt, Titan Robotics, Platypus, Robert Bosch RTC, American Sensors, Vocollect, Integrated Industrials Technology, Real Earth, HEBI Robotics, Near Earth, Coroware Test Labs, GE Fanuc, Science Applications International, Aethon, Applied Perception, Assistware Technology, Astrobotic Technology, Blue Belt Technologies, RE2, Discovery Robotics, Carnegie Robotics, Sensible Machines, Bosa Nova Robotics, Interbots, Accutronic, ARA, Composiflex, IbisTek, Neya Systems, QinetiQ, and Seegrid.

## Pittsburgh: A Leader in Self-Driving Vehicles

In 2017, the U.S. Department of Transportation named Pittsburgh as one of ten locations that will be designated as a National Proving

Ground for Automated Vehicle Technology, which enhances the city's position in the Autonomous Vehicle Technology industry.

Uber has headquartered its self-driving vehicle program in Pittsburgh and will invest $1 billion in the project. Uber is expected to have 1,000 local employees by 2018. Uber has made Pittsburgh the first city in the world to test self-driving taxis and they also operate a large, state-of-the-art test track in the city.

Ford Motor Company is investing $1 billion into Pittsburgh-based Argo AI to develop technology for its own self-driving vehicles. Argo AI plans to hire 200 additional employees in 2017, primarily in Pittsburgh. In addition, several other major automakers are exploring Pittsburgh for the same purpose, such as General Motors via NextDroid, as well as Delphi Automotive and Aurora Systems, who are hiring in Pittsburgh.

## Pittsburgh: A Leader in Marcellus and Utica Shale Production

It's been said by sources in the industry that there is more natural gas under western Pennsylvania than there is oil in Saudi Arabia. The Pittsburgh region has become a behemoth in the natural gas industry, particularly in the Marcellus and Utica shale area, creating an entire new industry in western Pennsylvania. Royal Dutch Shell is constructing a multi-billion-dollar ethane cracker plant to take advantage of these natural resources in the region. Pittsburgh is now considered the *Energy Capital of the East.*

Oil and gas companies have flocked to the region to create not only drilling sites, but regional offices and even plants. Below is a *partial* listing of companies that are listed as having presence in the Pittsburgh region include:

| | |
|---|---|
| Royal Dutch Shell | Range Resources |
| Chevron | EQT Corp. |
| CONSOL | Rice Energy |

| | |
|---|---|
| Chesapeake Energy | Chief Oil and Gas |
| Cabot Oil & Gas | Vantage Energy |
| Rex Energy | XTO Energy |
| Anadarko Petroleum | Energy Corp. of America |
| Noble Energy | |

**Pittsburgh has always maintained numerous Fortune 500 company headquarters and has played a major role in business and industry on a world-wide basis. A partial list of companies headquartered in Pittsburgh and/or have a significant presence in the region:**

| | |
|---|---|
| U.S. Steel | Bayer |
| ALCOA | Covestro |
| GNC | Calgon Carbon |
| Star Kist | Education Management |
| H.J. Heinz/Kraft | Federated Investors |
| PPG Industries | Rue21 |
| FedEx Ground | Highmark Health |
| Westinghouse | UPMC |
| American Eagle Outfitters | Koppers |
| Dick's Sporting Goods | Giant Eagle |
| PNC Bank | Howard Hanna Real Estate |
| Bank of New York-Mellon | CONSOL Energy |

| | |
|---|---|
| EQT | Allegheny Technologies |
| Ampco Pittsburgh | Nova Chemicals |
| Black Box | ModCloth |
| Mine Safety Appliance | Mylan |
| Lanxess | American Bridge |
| DQE | Medrad |
| 84 Lumber | Citizens Bank |
| Eat'n Park | Atlas Energy |
| Wabtec | Allegheny Energy |
| WESCO International | Dynavox |
| Kennemetal | RTI International Metals |
| ANSYS | Duolingo |

## FAMOUS "PITTSBURGHERS"

### *Actors/Hollywood*

| | |
|---|---|
| Michael Keaton | Sharon Stone |
| Gene Kelly | Jeff Goldblum |
| Jimmy Stewart | Charles Bronson |
| Shirley Jones | Joe Maganinello |
| David O. Selznick | Zachry Quinto |

Rob Marshall

Kathleen Marshall

Charles Grodin

F. Murray Abraham

Demi Moore

David Conrad

Julie Benz

Charles Esten

Gillian Jacobs

Lamman Rucker

Tom Atkins

Ted Cassidy

Fred Rogers

William Powell

Ming-Na

Martha Graham

Antoine Fuqua

Billy Gardell

Tom Savini

John Davidson

Frank Gorshin

Jack Dodson

Dennis Miller

Marty Allen

Steve Byrne

Joe Letteri

## Singers/Musicians

Christina Aguilera

Wiz Khalifa

Jackie Evancho

Perry Como

Bret Michaels

Bobby Vinton

Billy Eckstine

George Benson

Stephen Collins Foster

Henry Mancini

| | |
|---|---|
| B.E. Taylor | Daya |
| Earl "Fatha" Hines | Sarah Marince |
| Billy Porter | Ethelbert Nevin |
| Donnie Iris | Lou Christie |
| Walt Harper | Mac Miller |
| Joe Grushecky | The Vogues |
| Art Blakey | The Marcels |
| Mary Lou Metzger | Chris Jamison |
| Esteban | Jimmy Beaumont & The Skyliners |
| Erroll Garner | |

## *Authors*

| | |
|---|---|
| Nellie Bly | Willa Cather |
| Rachel Carson | David McCullough |
| Gertrude Stein | Michael Chabon |
| Stephen Chbosky | John Dickson Carr |
| August Wilson | |

## *Other Famous "Pittsburghers"*

| | |
|---|---|
| Andy Warhol (Artist) | Andrew Carnegie (Philanthropist) |

John Brashear (Astronomer)

Mary Cassat (Artist)

Mark Cuban (Philanthropist)

Porky Chedwick (Radio)

H.J. Heinz (Corporate Magnet)

Jonas Salk (Polio Vaccine Inventor)

Cardinal Donald Wuerl (Washington D.C.)

George Westinghouse (Industry Pioneer)

Andrew Mellon (Financier)

George C. Marshall (Five-Star General)

Derrick A. Bell (Law Professor)

Gertrude Stein (Artist)

Burton Morris (Artist)

Teenie Harris (Photographer)

George Sotter (Artist)

Naomi Sims (Model)

## FAMOUS ATHLETES AND SPORT FIGURES FROM PITTSBURGH – (PARTIAL LIST)

| Football | Bud Carson | Dan Rooney |
|---|---|---|
| Mike Ditka | Bill Cowher | Joe Namath |
| Dan Marino | Todd Haley | Tony Dorsett |
| Joe Montana | Jim Haslett | Curtis Martin |
| Johnny Unitas | Chuck Knox | Brandon Marshall |
| Jim Kelly | Sean Lee | Rasheed Marshall |
| George Blanda | Darrelle Revis | Jimbo Covert |
| Mike McCarthy | Art Rooney | Bill Fralic |

Rock DiLisio

Russ Grimm

Cameron Heyward

Randy White

Ty Law

Dick Nolan

Marty
Schottenheimer

Jim Tomsula

Joe Walton

Dave Wannstedt

Gus Ferrotte

Terry Hanratty

Barry Alvarez

Bob Davie

Charlie Batch

Todd Blackledge

Marc Bulger

Jeff Hostetler

Bruce Gradkowski

Beano Cook

## Baseball

Pie Trainor

Honus Wagner

Buddy Bell

Doc Medich

Dick Groat

Dick Allen

Neil Walker

Sid Bream

Sean Casey

Bill Mazeroski

Don Kelly

Stan Musial

Ken Griffey, Sr.

Ken Griffey, Jr.

Bobby Wallace

Terry Francona

Art Howe

Ken Macha

## Basketball

George Karl

Suzie
McConnell-Serio

Sean Miller

Skip Prosser

Herb Sendek

DeJaun Blair

Swin Cash

Danny Fortson

Armen Gilliam

Billy Knight

Maurice Lucas

T.J. McConnell

## Hockey

Brandon Saad

Ryan Malone

R.J. Umberger

John Gibson

Vincent Trocheck

| | | |
|---|---|---|
| Matt Bartkowski | Rocco Mediate | **Boxing** |
| Mike Weber | **Soccer** | Billy Conn |
| Dylan Reese | Meghan Klingenberg | Michael Moorer |
| Bill Thomas | **Wrestling** | Paul Spadafora |
| **Golf** | Bruno Sammartino | |
| Arnold Palmer | Kurt Angle | |

# THE FOLLOWING WERE INVENTED OR HAD THEIR "FIRSTS" IN PITTSBURGH

Pittsburgh is unique in many ways, including being the only city with an entrance (Fort Pitt Tunnel) and the city with the most vehicle carrying bridges in the world (446). Pittsburgh has had many "firsts", including where the first humans lived in the United States, the first radio broadcasts, the first movie theater and, yes, even where the first flight took place. The "firsts" continue with Pittsburgh being the first city to have self-driving cars. Here's a list of more:

**First Human Habitation in the United States:** Paleo-Indians – 19,000 years ago – Meadowcroft Rock Shelter

**World's First Commercial Radio Station:** KDKA Radio – November 1920

**World's First Commercial Radio Broadcast:** KDKA Radio – Harding-Cox presidential election returns – November 2, 1920

**World's First Radio Broadcast of a Baseball Game:** KDKA Radio – Philadelphia vs. Pittsburgh – August 4, 1921

**World's First Radio Broadcast of a Church Service:** KDKA Radio – January 2, 1921

**World's First Radio Broadcast of a Phonograph Record**: Frank Conrad – Private Station – October 17, 1919

**World's First Movie Theater – Nickelodeon**: Smithfield Street (Downtown) – June 19, 1905

**Worlds' First Movies Shown in a Movie Theater**: *Poor But Honest* and *The Baffled Burglar* – Nickelodeon – Downtown – June 1905

**First Public Library:** Carnegie Library of Pittsburgh – Created by Andrew Carnegie – February 1890

**First Gas Station:** Gulf Oil Corporation – East Liberty section of City – December 1913

**First Road Map:** Gulf Oil Corporation – Allegheny County – March 1914

**World's First Picture Phone Use:** Mayor Flaherty to John Harper of ALCOA – June 30, 1970

**World's First Ferris Wheel:** Invented by G.W. Ferris for the Chicago's Word's Fair - 1892

**First in Flight:** Gustave Whitehead – Half Mile Flight – May 1899

**First Air Mail Flight**: Plane – Miss Pittsburgh – April 1927

**First Steamboat** – Built in Pittsburgh - 1811

**First City to have Self-Driving Cars:** Self-Driving Taxis – Uber - 2016

# Chapter 14

# THE MYTHS OF PITTSBURGH

## THE WEATHER IN PITTSBURGH IS NOT SO GREAT.

If you're looking for a location with comfortable summers, nice springs, great falls and average winters, then Pittsburgh certainly has the weather for you. Especially summer and fall, which are very comfortable seasons in western Pennsylvania. Pittsburgh's weather is underrated and after reading the following, you'll understand why:

(The following information is from the National Oceanic and Atmospheric Administration (NOAA) and the United States Commerce Department)

Pittsburgh sits in what is called the Allegheny Plateau Climate Division of western Pennsylvania, which also includes eastern Ohio and northern West Virginia. In Pittsburgh, this area is often referred to as the "Tri-State Area."

People often equate Pittsburgh as a snowy or rainy locale, but if you read the following you will see that there is little to no basis to such a perception – when compared to many other locations across the United States.

The first thing that the "Weather Worriers" of the world need to realize is that snow is not a disaster (unless it falls in significant amounts in a short-period of time) and Pittsburgh rarely receives such snowfalls. On the other hand, the southern and western portions of the United States do experience life-threatening and property destructing weather disasters frequently, such as hurricanes, tropical storms, exorbitant heat, earthquakes, tornados, floods, wildfires, mudslides and droughts. None of which are a major threat to the Pittsburgh area.

**Winter:**

Pittsburgh is often said to have bad winters. In all reality, they are very mild when compared to other Northeastern and Midwestern locations. Pittsburgh's winter weather is changing, which is proven by the fact that it has experienced five of its warmest winters just in the past 20 years (1998, 2002, 2012, 2016 and 2017). Four of the warmest winters on record have occurred within the past sixteen years and three of those winters have occurred in the past five years. The recent winters of 2016 and 2017 were extremely mild with far above average temperatures and far below average snowfalls.

Pittsburgh rarely receives a significant snowfall at one time. As of this writing, the last time that Pittsburgh had 10 or more inches of snow in a one or two-day period was 2010. The previous snowfall of 10 inches or more was in 1994. Typically, the area receives snowfalls of below 3 inches.

Here's the proof of Pittsburgh's mild winters, which comes from some of the most highly regarded sources in the country. See if you notice Pittsburgh on any of the lists below.

Per *Forbes Magazine*, these are the **Worst Weather Cities** in the United States:
1. Cleveland
2. Boston
3. New York City
4. Milwaukee
5. Chicago
6. Minneapolis

7. Indianapolis
8. Columbus
9. Detroit
10. Baltimore

Per _Weather.com_ in 2014, these are the **Worst Weather Locations** in the United States:
1. Toledo, Ohio
2. Chicago
3. Detroit
4. Billings, Montana
5. Ft. Wayne, Indiana
6. Peoria, Illinois
7. Grand Rapids, Michigan
8. Duluth, Minnesota
9. Green Bay, Wisconsin
10. Minneapolis/St. Paul

Per _Weather.com_, these are the **Snowiest Cities** in the United States:
1. Syracuse, New York
2. Erie, Pennsylvania
3. Rochester, New York
4. Buffalo
5. Boulder, Colorado
6. Anchorage, Alaska
7. Grand Rapids, Michigan
8. Cleveland
9. South Bend, Indiana
10. Worchester, Massachusetts

Actually, when it comes to the amount of snowfall per city on the last list - Pittsburgh isn't even in the Top 20. Pittsburgh's snowfall averages 29 inches per year. The average US city (nationwide) accumulates 25 inches of snow per year, again showing Pittsburgh as having average winters. The preconceived idea that Pittsburgh is very snowy locale is simply not substantiated.

**What about Cold?**

If you believe that Pittsburgh's temperature is cold when compared to other cities in the United States, think again:

- Per USAToday, Pittsburgh isn't in the *Top 50 Coldest Cities* in the U.S. and
- Per City-Data.com, Pittsburgh isn't in the *Top 101 Coldest Cities in the United States* with populations over 50,000.

The above statistics from highly-regarded sources prove that Pittsburgh winters are somewhat over-hyped with a preconceived perception that is not based on factual statistics.

**Summer in Pittsburgh**

Pittsburgh is known to have comfortable and mild summers, though it experienced one of its warmest summers in 2016. Generally, Pittsburgh experiences mild summers, but the climate of this area is considered "Hot Continental" and includes frequent inversions of air from the Gulf of Mexico during the summer. This may result in spells of warm weather (with humidity). This actually sounds like the climate of Florida, but without the exorbitant heat and humidity and the constant threat of hurricanes.

Actually, some residents of Pittsburgh go south for the winter and return to Pittsburgh from spring through the holidays, because the weather is generally much more pleasant than the overwhelming heat, humidity and hurricane threat of the southern United States. Many residents of the southern U.S. also look to avoid such harsh weather and come to the Pittsburgh area during the summer months.

- This is not unusual and it's substantiated by:
1. the *Places Rated Almanac* calling Pittsburgh a great place for a summer home (based on its mild summers) and
2. Pittsburgh ranked as the #10 location in the United States for "Best Summers" on a recent *Forbes* list.

*USA Today* and *Sperling's Best Places* rated the following U.S. cities as having the *best* summer weather, due to low heat indexes:
1. Seattle
2. Portland
3. San Francisco
4. Denver
5. San Jose
6. Salt Lake City
7. Milwaukee
8. Detroit
9. Pittsburgh

"These locations have comfortable climates, comfortable summers, low heat indexes and low health risks associated with heat."

The following locations have the *worst* summers in the United States:

Per *Sperling's Best Places*, the **Worst Summer Weather** in the United States is located in:
1. Phoenix
2. Las Vegas
3. Dallas
4. Houston
5. Austin, Texas
6. San Antonio
7. Miami
8. New Orleans
9. Orlando
10. Tampa

"Avoid places, such as these, due to high heat indexes, which are attributable to heat-related mortality."

**It Rains Too Much in Pittsburgh**

Per Sperling, Pittsburgh actually receives below average U.S. rainfall at 36 inches of rain per year. The average U.S. city receives 37 inches of rain per year.

Pittsburgh is often criticized for receiving a lot of rain, but who actually has the *most* rain in the United States?

Per the U.S. Government's NOAA and USATravel, the **Most Rain and Precipitation Cities** in the United States are:
1. New Orleans
2. Miami
3. Birmingham, Alabama
4. Memphis
5. Jacksonville, Florida
6. Orlando
7. New York City
8. Houston
9. Atlanta
10. Nashville

When you combine rain and snow precipitation, Pittsburgh moves into the Top 10 on the precipitation list, but it has plenty of company from cities in Florida and other supposed "sunny" locales. Actually, the rainiest state in the country is Hawaii.

**Pittsburgh is Often Cloudy**

Days that are recorded as "cloudy" are actually not as cloudy as they may seem – per the NOAA descriptions below. Notice that days considered "Cloudy" and "Mostly Cloudy," can include anywhere between three to five hours of sunshine during that same day (or up to 50% sunshine), but go into the records as *cloudy days*. If the sun was out in that location for as long as five hours that particular day – the records will show that the day was "mostly cloudy." On days where the sun could shine for as long as <u>seven hours</u> (or have up to 70% sunshine) the records will show that the day is officially "Partly Cloudy."

**Overcast** - 1 hour or less sunshine recorded for the day or 10% sunshine

**Cloudy** - 3 hours or less sunshine or 30% sunshine

**Mostly Cloudy** - 3-5 hours of sunshine or between 30-50% sunshine

**Partly Cloudy** - 5-7 hours of sunshine or between 50-70% sunshine

**Mostly Sunny** - over 7 hours of sunshine or over 70% sunshine

**Clear** - no more than 1/8th of the sky obscured at any time during the day.

❖ Per Sperling, the cloudiest cities in the United States are:
  • Seattle
  • Portland
  • Buffalo

Per Sperling, Pittsburgh has an average of 162 days of Mostly Sunny, Partly Sunny or Clear weather per year – that's 70% or more sunshine on those days. The remainder of the days has the word "cloudy" associated with them ranking Pittsburgh in the higher end of overall cloudy days per city. Considering the above, most of those supposedly "cloudy" days could have anywhere between 30 to 70% sunshine, but are officially recorded as "cloudy" per the definition.

❖ To show the misperception of "cloudy days":
❖ Per Sperling, cities with the most Partially Cloudy days in the United States:
  ➢ Miami, Florida
  ➢ Orlando, Florida
  ➢ Tampa, Florida
  ➢ Denver, Colorado
  ➢ Jacksonville, Florida

**Weather as a Natural Disaster**

Another factor you have to consider is the propensity of an area to have natural disasters, typically caused by the weather. Unlike many areas in Florida and the Carolinas that are under constant hurricane threat through many months of the year, Pittsburgh doesn't have these life threatening and property destructing events to worry about. Pittsburgh is also not subject to earthquakes, constant tornados, drought, mudslides, wildfires or exorbitant heat, as much of the southern and western portions of the United States encounter.

Per NBC News, the following states have the most natural disasters:
1. Texas
2. California
3. Oklahoma
4. New York
5. Florida
6. Louisiana
7. Alabama
8. Kentucky
9. Arkansas
10. Missouri

If you break down the U.S. cities with the worst potential for natural disaster, they all happen to be in Florida, California or Texas.

Even though Pittsburgh has three rivers, flooding is not a constant threat. The last time that the rivers overflowed the banks with any significance in Pittsburgh was in the year *1936*. It is a known fact that almost every state in the U.S. experiences flooding.

Per CBS, below is a list of the **"Safest" Major U.S. Cities** from Natural Disasters:
1. Syracuse
2. Cleveland
3. Buffalo
4. Chicago

5. Denver
6. Detroit

Though these are the safest cities, many consider snow or significant snow as a natural disaster. Snow – in heavy snowfalls – can be a significant hindrance to daily life. If that is factored into the "disaster" equation, then all of the above-listed cities are no longer the "safest" in the United States.

For Example:

*Syracuse* is listed as the safest city from natural disaster, but is also listed as the #1 "Snowiest" city in the United States. *Cleveland* is listed as the second safest city in the U.S., but is listed as the #1 Worst Weather City and the 8th Snowiest. *Buffalo*, *Chicago* and *Detroit* are also in the Top 10 Snowiest Cities in the United States and Denver also receives significant snowfalls.

**Pittsburgh: One of America's Safest Cities from Natural Disaster**

Natural disasters are caused by the weather or involve weather-related factors. Per the analysis provided by the Langley Group and the University of Pittsburgh:

The Pittsburgh region is relatively immune to natural disasters. Pittsburgh's geological location precludes the occurrence of many kinds of natural disasters. Pittsburgh is far enough from a coast so that hurricanes have little or no effect. Ecologically, Pittsburgh has a very low likelihood of wildfires, mudslides and other natural disasters. The National Disaster Risk Map, produced by the National Disaster Coalition, graphically depicts the areas of the United States that are prone to certain classes of disaster. Pittsburgh is among the safest U.S. locations for natural disasters.

**Please view the map at: cnp.pitt.edu/certificate/papers/ jrcpgheconqtrly.doc**

The map clearly depicts that Pittsburgh is safe from threats of hurricanes, earthquakes, tornados, floods, wildfires, mudslides, tsunami and volcanos. Pittsburgh is also a safe locale from extreme heat and even regular, heavy snowfalls.

Most of the safest cities in the United States are located near the Great Lakes (Cleveland, Chicago, Buffalo, Syracuse and Detroit). Pittsburgh is also in the Great Lakes region (near Lake Erie). Per the natural disaster map provided by the National Disaster Coalition, Pittsburgh is one of America's safest cities from natural disaster and is not in the Top 20 "Snowiest" cities in the United States (unlike all of the other cities on the "Safest" list, which are in the Top 10 of "Snowiest Cities"). Thus, if you combine safety from natural disaster and factor in heavy snowfalls and extreme heat as a natural disaster - Pittsburgh just may be the safest city in the United States from all forms of natural disasters.

# IS PITTSBURGH REALLY AMERICA'S MOST LIVABLE CITY?

Beyond the incredible cultural amenities, great food, incredible views, outdoor meccas and friendly people, Pittsburgh has a low cost-of-living, low crime rate, affordable housing and a re-born economy. Beyond that, it offers free college education to its city students and is in a State that doesn't tax the likes of food and clothing, nor does it tax its senior citizens on their pensions or social security. The following list from some of the world's most renowned publications is all that really needs said on the subject:

- Pittsburgh: **Top 40 Cities to Live in the World (2017)** – The Economist
- Pittsburgh: **Best Places to Live (2016)** – Men's Journal Magazine
- Pittsburgh: **Most Livable Place in the Continental United States** – *The Economist Magazine*
- Pittsburgh: **One of the most Livable Places in the World and Best in the U.S.** – *The Economist Magazine*

- Pittsburgh: **One of the World's 11 Best & Most Livable Cities (2015)** – Metropolis Magazine
- Pittsburgh: **Most Livable U.S. City** – Forbes Magazine
- Pittsburgh: **The Most Livable City** – BestPlaces.net
- Pittsburgh: **Most Livable City in the U.S.** – Rand McNally
- Pittsburgh: **Most Livable City in the U.S.** (Twice) – Places Rated Almanac

# PITTSBURGH IS A SMALL CITY?

Pittsburgh is by no means a small city. Pittsburgh is actually one of the largest cities in the country if it would be allowed to structure itself like most of the other cities in the United States. Allegheny County, the county that Pittsburgh is in, has a population of over 1.2 million people and the metropolitan statistical area has 2.4 million residents. If Pittsburgh had enacted expansion and annexation as many other cities have and encompassed its entire county, Pittsburgh would have over 1,000,000 residents and be one of the Top Ten Largest Cities in United States.

Most, if not many, cities in the country encompass their entire county for purposes of population and land mass. Pittsburgh, on the other hand, is only 1 of 130 municipalities in Allegheny County and only the actual population of the city proper counts as Pittsburgh's population. Only one other county in the entire country has more municipalities than Allegheny County – Cook County, Illinois. The population of the remainder of the county does not count towards Pittsburgh's population, even though Allegheny County is one of the most populous counties in the country. It is well-known that Allegheny County residents – and even some surrounding counties – consider themselves to be from Pittsburgh, even if they do not actually live within the city borders.

In most cities, those 130 municipalities would become one city via concurred annexation. This has been done over and over across the country, but laws prohibit such annexation in Pennsylvania and legislative approval would be needed to institute it. Annexation is very prominent in other parts of the country, leading to automatic population gains without the need of increased citizenship within their original city borders. The city borders are expanded, thus inheriting population growth. Many cities are currently exploring further annexation of surrounding communities to expand their borders.

Land Expansion of America's Ten Largest Cities from 1910 to 2000 (Per the U.S. Census Bureau):
- New York – 6% expansion to 303 square miles
- Los Angeles – 472% expansion to 469 square miles
- Chicago – 23% expansion to 227 square miles
- Houston – 3,329% expansion to 579 square miles
- Philadelphia – 4% expansion to 135 square miles
- Phoenix – 2,677% expansion to 475 square miles
- San Diego – 226% expansion to 324 square miles
- Dallas – 2,014% expansion to 343 square miles
- San Antonio – 1,039% expansion to 408 square miles
- Detroit – 240% expansion to 139 square miles

Pittsburgh, compared to the above, is only 55 square miles, while Allegheny County is over 730 square miles. If Pittsburgh encompassed the entire county, as many cities do, it would be larger in land mass than any of the top ten cities. Pittsburgh has expanded 34% in the same time period (1910 to 2000) but only to reach 55 square miles. As can be seen, Philadelphia, another Pennsylvania city, has expanded the least of any of the above cities, further depicting Pennsylvania laws restricting expansion.

Philadelphia, though, is already 135 square miles and it encompasses the entire county where it sits (Philadelphia County). Again, Pittsburgh is only 1 of 130 municipalities in Allegheny County. Even so, Pittsburgh has one of the highest populations per square miles in the country at 6,017. That's more than Houston, Phoenix, San Diego, Dallas and San Antonio – all Top 10 most populous U.S. cities.

Pittsburgh is currently the 63$^{rd}$ largest city in the United States, primarily due to its geographical structure. To show the discrepancies of being 1 of 130 municipalities in one county, Allegheny County is one of the Top 30 most populous counties in the country. Pittsburgh's Standard Metropolitan Statistical Area is the 22$^{nd}$ largest in the United States.

Pittsburgh's population would even be much greater had it not suffered through the loss of the steel industry in the 1970's and 1980's. A large portion of the population was lost due to this economic downturn. Within the past ten years, Pittsburgh's population has shown stability for the first time since the downturn, primarily due to its resurgence as a mecca for technology, healthcare, education and the natural gas industry.

In 2017, legislation is being proposed to allow municipalities in Allegheny County to disincorporate. Should certain municipalities choose to do so they will be absorbed by the county and possibly be allowed to merge with an adjoining municipality. This may be the first step in allowing Pittsburgh to grow through a means that many other cities have taken advantage of over and over.

**Pittsburgh: The City of Bridges**

Pittsburgh has 446 bridges, which is more than any city in the world. These bridges are primarily vehicle carrying. Technically, Venice, Italy has more bridges, but none are vehicle carrying, nor are they anywhere near the size of those in Pittsburgh.

Having three rivers in a metropolitan area lends itself to the need of so many bridges.

# IS PITTSBURGH THE HOLLYWOOD OF THE EAST?

Pittsburgh has been called *Hollywood of the East* by leading news sources, such as Entertainment Weekly (EW) and CNN. In less than a decade, over 40 feature films have been made in Pittsburgh, as well as numerous television series. Several casting companies are headquartered or have opened offices in Pittsburgh and local employment in the industry has skyrocketed. In addition, the Screen Actors Guild (SAG-AFTRA) operates an office in Downtown Pittsburgh and local production studios have opened and more are in the planning stages. Adding to the local industry, two Pittsburgh universities, Carnegie Mellon and Point Park, have established an excellent national reputation for film acting and studies. Carnegie Mellon alone is the alma mater of: Zachary Quinto, Ted Danson, Matt Bomer, Holly Hunter, Blair Underwood, Joe Manganiello, Josh Gad, Ethan Hawke, George Peppard, George Romero, James Cromwell, Jack Klugman, Rob Marshall, Steven Bonchco, Megan Hilty and Barbara Feldon – to name but a few. Of course, David O. Selznick, who produced the ultimate movie classic, *Gone With the Wind*, was born in Pittsburgh. (See a list of actors from the Pittsburgh area in the previous chapter)

The Pittsburgh Film Office is the catalyst in attracting feature film and TV productions and Pennsylvania's Film Tax Credits have helped significantly. Together, they have created an entire industry bringing jobs and commerce to Pittsburgh and western Pennsylvania. Pittsburgh is certainly not new the film industry and its movie-making history is significant.

The world's first movie theater and first movies were shown in Pittsburgh and it is the birthplace of MGM and Warner Brothers Studios. For decades, Pittsburgh was also a major screening location for all of the major motion pictures studios. Pittsburgh's movie history continued with Academy Award films being shot in the city and region, such as *The Deer Hunter, Silence of the Lambs* and *Flashdance*. In present day, the city has become a major force in movie production with films such as, *The Dark Knight Rises, Fences, Perks of Being a Wallflower, Foxcatcher* and *Jack Reacher.*

Soon, movie theater history will be showcased, as Pittsburgh will be the home of the Theatre Historical Society of America, which moved to the city in 2017 from Chicago. Pittsburgh was chosen over 38 cities for the museum, which is the archive of the nation's largest research and preservation resources for items pertaining to movie theaters and their social and historical significance.

- **Pittsburgh is where the first movie theater was located – The Nickelodeon**

In 1905, the city was home to the world's first theater dedicated solely to moving pictures. Located on Smithfield Street in Downtown Pittsburgh, the "Nickelodeon" was opened by John Harris and Harry Davis. The name "Nickelodeon" – which was combination of the words "nickel" (referring to the 5 cents cost of entrance) and "odeon," which is a Greek term for theater – became the name of choice for theaters for many years.

The Nickelodeon was an immediate success and it is said that as many as 7,000 people a day visited the 100-seat theater. The first movies shown at the world's first movie theater were *Poor But Honest* and *The Baffled Burglar.* Due to its great success, Davis and Harris eventually opened 18 other Nickelodeons throughout the city.

- **Warner Brothers Studios began in Pittsburgh**

Harry and Albert Warner relocated from Ohio to Pittsburgh to become involved with the nickelodeon movie industry. In 1906, they launched the Duquesne Amusement film exchange company, which was very successful. They eventually sold their company and created Warner Brothers Studios.

- **MGM Studios began in Pittsburgh**

In 1910, two men from Pittsburgh, Richard Rowland and James Clark, created a local film exchange under the name of Rowland & Clark. The General Film Corporation purchased their business and the two used their proceeds to open several opulent theaters in the Pittsburgh area. Richard Rowland then created the Metro Film Company, which eventually merged with two California companies – Goldwyn Pictures and the Louis B. Mayer Company – creating Metro-Goldwyn-Mayer (MGM).

- **Pittsburgh played a significant role as a major film exchange**

In the early years of film-making, Pittsburgh was a major film exchange for all of major motion film studios. Film exchanges screened newly produced films to determine their potential release to theaters. From the 1920s through the 1950s, the Boulevard of the Allies in Downtown Pittsburgh was home to offices, screening rooms and film libraries for MGM, Paramount Pictures, Columbia Pictures, United Artists and Universal Pictures. In present day, the Paramount Building is still intact and carries the signature Paramount logo above the entrance. The building is under preservation.

# MOVIES FILMED IN PITTSBURGH (AND SURROUNDING AREA)

- **The List below includes movies filmed in full (or partially) in the Pittsburgh area**

### Academy Award Winning Films (in some category)

**Fences** – Danzel Washington, Viola Davis

**The Deer Hunter** – Meryl Streep, Robert De Niro

**Silence of the Lambs** – Jodie Foster, Anthony Hopkins

**Flashdance** – Jennifer Beals, Michael Nouri

### Recently Filmed in Pittsburgh

**The Dark Knight Rises** – Christian Bale, Tom Hardy, Michael Caine

**Jack Reacher** – Tom Cruise, Robert Duvall, Rosamund Pike

**Fences** – Denzel Washington, Viola Davis

**Perks of Being a Wallflower** – Logan Lerman, Emma Watson

The Fault in Our Stars – Shailene Woodley, Ansel Egort, Laura Dern

Concussion – Will Smith, Alec Baldwin

Foxcatcher – Steve Carell, Mark Ruffalo, Channing Tatum, Sienna Miller

Love and Other Drugs – Jake Gyllenhaal, Anne Hathaway

American Pastoral – Ewan McGregor, Jennifer Connelly

Love the Coopers – John Goodman, Diane Keaton, Olivia Wilde, Alan Arkin, Amanda Seyfried, Ed Helms, Marisa Tomei, Anthony Mackie, Jake Lacy

Last Flag Flying – Bryan Cranston, Steve Carrell, Lawrence Fishburne

Where'd You Go, Bernadette? – Cate Blanchette, Kristen Wiig

Unstoppable – Danzel Washington, Chris Pine, Rosario Dawson, Mimi Rogers

Fathers and Daughters – Russell Crowe, Amanda Seyfried, Aaron Paul

Avengers (partially shot) – Robert Downey, Jr. Chis Evans, Chris Hemsworth, Scarlett Johansson, Mark Ruffalo

The Last Witch Hunter – Vin Diesel

Out of the Furnace – Chirstian Bale, Casey Affleck, Zoe Saldana, Forest Whitaker, Willem Dafoe, Woody Harrelson

Southpaw – Jake Gyllenhaal, Rachel McAdams, Forest Whitaker

Me & Earl (and the Dying Girl)– Thomas Mann, Olivia Cooke

Promised Land – Matt Damon, John Krasinski, Hal Holbrook, Frances McDormand

Warrior – Tom Hardy, Nick Nolte, Kurt Angle

Abduction – Taylor Lautner, Signorney Weaver, Alfred Molina

The Next Three Days – Russell Crowe, Liam Neeson, Elizabeth Banks, Brian Dennehy

One for the Money – Katherine Heigel

**Won't Back Down** – Maggie Gyllenhaal, Holly Hunter

**Unsinkable** – Emily Lapisardi, Daina Griffith

**I Am Number Four** – Timothy Olyphant

**She's Out of My League** – Jay Brauchel, Alice Eve

**Adventureland** – Kristen Stewart, Ryan Reynolds, Kristen Wiig, Jesse Eisenberg

**My Bloody Valentine** – Jensen Ackles, Jamie King

**Zack and Miri** – Seth Rogen, Elizabeth Banks, Kevin Smith

**Smart People** – Thomas Church, Dennis Quaid, Sarah Jessica Parker, Ellen Page

**The Road** – Viggo Mortensen, Robert Duvall, Charlize Theron

**The Lifeguard** – Kristen Bell

**Shelter** – Julianne Moore

**On the Inside** – Olivia Wilde

**Sorority Row** – Carrie Fisher

**Dog Jack** – Louis Gossett, Jr.

**Hollywood & Wine** – Chris Kattan, David Spade

**Shannon's Rainbow** – Louis Gossett, Jr., Daryl Hannah, Charles Durning

**Homecoming** – Mischa Barton, Jessica Stroup

• This is a partial list of movies filmed in Pittsburgh

## MOVIES FILMED IN THE RECENT PAST

**All the Right Moves** – Tom Cruise, Lea Thompson, Craig T. Nelson

**Mrs. Soffel** – Mel Gibson, Diane Keaton

**Gung Ho** – Michael Keaton

**Diabolique** – Sharon Stone

**Desperate Measures** – Michael Keaton, Andy Garcia

**Dogma** – Ben Affleck, Matt Damon, Salma Hayek

**Robocop** – Peter Weller

**Lorenzo's Oil** – Nick Nolte, Susan Sarandon, Laura Linney

**Ground Hog Day** – Bill Murray, Andie McDowell

**Striking Distance** – Bruce Willis, Dennis Farina, Sarah Jessica Parker

**Sudden Death** – Jean-Claude Van Damme

**Kingpin** – Bill Murray, Woody Harrelson, Randy Quaid

**Lady Beware** – Diane Lane, Michael Woods

**Slap Shot** – Paul Newman

**Dominick & Eugene** – Ray Liotta and Jamie Lee Curtis

**Waterland** – Ethan Hawke, Jeremy Irons

**Inspector Gadget** – Matthew Broderick, Dabney Coleman

**Wonder Boys** – Michael Douglas, Tobey Maguire, Robert Downey, Jr.

**The Mothman Prophecies** – Richard Gere, Debra Messing

**10th & Wolf** – Dennis Hopper, Brian Dennehy, Val Kilmer, Tommy Lee

**Mysteries of Pittsburgh** – Nick Nolte, Sienna Miller

**Innocent Blood** – Angela Bassett, Don Rickles, Anthony LaPaglia

**Pittsburgh** – Jeff Goldblum, Conan O'Brien, Ed Begley, Jr.

**Hoffa** – Jack Nicholson, Danny DeVito

**Eye of the Beholder** – Ewan McGregor, Ashley Judd

**The Cemetery Club** – Diane Ladd, Ellen Burstyn, Danny Aiello, Olympia Dukakis

**Timecop** – Jean Claude Van Demme

**Roommates** – Peter Falk, Julianne Moore

**Milk Money** – Melanie Griffith, Ed Harris

**Only You** – Robert Downey, Jr, Marisa Tomei

**Houseguest** – Sinbad, Phil Hartman

**Knightriders** – Ed Harris, Gary Lahti Night of the Living Dead, Duane Jones, Judith O'Dea

**Dawn of the Dead** – Tom Savini

**Creepshow** – Hal Holbrook, Ted Danson, E.G. Marshall, Leslie Nielson, Adrienne Barbeau

**The Fish that Saved Pittsburgh** – Jonathan Winters, Stockard Channing, Flip Wilson
- **This is a partial list of movies filmed in Pittsburgh**

## OTHER MOVIES FILMED IN PITTSBURGH

**Allegheny Uprising** – John Wayne

**Pittsburgh** – John Wayne, Marlene Dietrich

**Some Came Running** – Frank Sinatra, Dean Martin, Shirley MacLaine

**Angels in the Outfield** – Bing Crosby

**Pat and Mike** – Katherine Hepburn, Spencer Tracy

**The Rat Race** – Tony Curtis, Debbie Reynolds, Don Rickles

**Sylvia** – Peter Lawford

**The Winning Team** – Ronald Reagan, Doris Day

**The Legend of Johnny Appleseed** – Dennis Day

**The Unconquered** – Helen Keller, Gertrude Stein
- **This is a partial list of movies filmed in Pittsburgh**

## TELEVISION SHOWS FILMED IN PITTSBURGH

Besides becoming a mecca for movie-making, Pittsburgh has also become a haven for television filming also. Television shows recently filming their entire series in the city are:
- Mindhunter (Netflix)
- Gone (NBC Universal)
- Banshee (Cinemax)
- The Outsiders (WGN)
- Downward Dog (ABC)
- Dance Moms (Lifetime)
- Supah Ninjas (Nickelodeon)
- The Kill Point (Spike)
- Those Who Kill (LMN)
- Mulligan (Cable/Streaming)
- In addition, several network pilots have been filmed in the city.

Of course, the famous PBS series - Mister Rodgers Neighborhood - was filmed in Pittsburgh and the current series - Daniel Tiger's Neighborhood – is also produced in the city. A recent NBC television movie – Elixir – was also filmed in Pittsburgh.
- **For More Information of the Pittsburgh Film Industry, please visit the Pittsburgh Film Office Website: pghfilm.org**

# Chapter 15

# THE HISTORY OF PITTSBURGH

## HISTORY OF PITTSBURGH

### The French and Indian War and Early History

In early history, Native Americans inhabited the Pittsburgh region. History shows that as far back as 19,000 years ago Paleo-Indians lived in the area making the Pittsburgh area the first known location of human habitation in the United States. This is proven by evidence at an ongoing archaeological dig, southwest of Pittsburgh (Avella, PA), known as the Meadowcroft Rockshelter. Post the Paleo-Indian period, the Mound Builder Indians lived in the region constructing their signature Mounds during what is called the Adena culture period. A Mound still exists less than a mile from Downtown Pittsburgh in McKees Rocks, PA. During the 1700's, the region was controlled by the Iroquois Nation. The tribes that inhabited the Pittsburgh area primarily included the Shawnee and the Delaware (known also as the Lenape). Other tribes known to be in the region included the Senaca, Mohawk, Mohican, Cayuga, Wyandot, Tisagechroami and Oneida.

Later in the 1700's the French and Indian war began. The French and Indian War can be said to be the first true *world war* and was part of a larger imperial war between Great Britain and France known as the Seven Years War. The British and their American colonies fought a long battle against the French and their Native American Indian allies. The entire war was primarily fought over the control of one piece of land at the forks of the Allegheny, Monongahela and Ohio Rivers, in what is now the City of Pittsburgh in the State of Pennsylvania.

Let it be said that there is no other single piece of ground that has been so sought after and coveted than that triangular passage way to the west. The powers of the world, namely Britain and France, fought ferociously for from 1755 until 1763 for the right to control what is now known as the "Point."

The hostilities between the world powers began in the 1740's, when the French sent an expedition of 230 armed men from Canada, under the command of Captain Pierre-Joseph Celoron de Blainville, down the Ohio River and into western Pennsylvania, for purposes of claiming the land as French holdings. This would be done by the contingent burying lead plates in the ground stating the French claim to the land. Captain de Blainville also expelled ten British traders in Logstown, and any others in the area, and warned the Ohio River Valley Indians not to trade with them. When he returned to Canada, Captain de Blainville reported that it would be necessary to build a fortified military route through the valley in order to control it.

The tensions increased when, in the early 1750's, the French began to establish a string of forts west of the Allegheny Mountains. In 1752, the Marquis Duquesne was made governor-general of New France and set out to construct forts at Presque Island (Shores of Lake Erie) and Rivere aux Boefs (Waterford, near the Allegheny River). The French intended to keep these western lands or the Ohio Valley, in the hands of French citizens for the purposes of fur trapping and, secondly, in order to deter the land-hungry American colonists from venturing into the area.

At approximately the same time in 1749, the King of England bestowed a massive land grant to a group of Virginians, called the Ohio Company, for lands in the Ohio valley for purposes including "…erecting forts within the king's own territory." A charter secured 200,000 acres of land near the forks of the Ohio River. Their intention was also to control the western lands, and to successfully continue in the lucrative fur trade. Obviously, tensions mounted as both the French and Britain's American colonists, moved into the same area with similar goals.

Of course, the land that was in contention was inhabited by the native Indian tribes, namely, the Shawnee, Delaware and Lenape nations, and their initial reaction was to side with one of the contending powers. Most of the tribes tended to favor the French, since French traders did not intend to create a large number of settlements, unlike the British. The tribes also saw the French as conducting business more fairly than the British. The Indians had been known to ally with the French in other land control disputes, and this ensuing conflict was no different.

Current day western Pennsylvania and Pittsburgh were in the Virginia colony and not Pennsylvania. Robert Dinwiddie, Virginia lieutenant governor and member of the Ohio Company, found the French fort incursion in the western lands offensive. He summonsed a small group of men and dispatched them into the disputed territory with the intent of delivering a letter of protest to French officials, and asking them to vacate the area. In 1753, a young man named George Washington led the group to their destination.

During the long 900 mile journey to Fort LeBoeuf, Washington spotted a very strategic piece of land at the confluence of the Allegheny and Monongahela Rivers, where they met to form the mighty Ohio (present-day Pittsburgh). He noted in his journal on November 22, 1753, "As I got down before the canoe, I spent some time viewing the rivers and the land in the fork, which I think extremely well situated for a fort...as it has absolute command of the rivers." This sighting was the most successful portion of the journey, for the French, once confronted, refused to leave the Ohio valley.

Based upon George Washington's reports and recommendations, the land at the confluence of the three rivers greatly interested the British. They realized that not only was the location on the furthest fringes of westward expansion, but the rivers also opened up a swift gateway to the vast land and riches which lay beyond. In early 1754, officials sent a small force to the site where they began to construct Fort Prince George in order to claim and control the continent's most strategic location. Before construction could be completed, the French, still very present in the area, sent a much larger contingent of 500 men, and forced the British, under the command of Ensign Edward Ward, to abandon their task and return home. The French proceeded to complete the partially constructed fort, named it Fort Duquesne, after the Marquis Duquesne, and now claimed control over the *gateway to the west*.

At approximately the same time, Governor Dinwiddie of Virginia, based on the British's decision to construct a fort at the confluence of the three rivers, felt it necessary that they take advantage of the situation and assist in expelling the French from western Pennsylvania. He sought assistance from the other colonies, but was refused. He then turned again to twenty-two-year-old George Washington, who led the Virginia militia into the disputed Ohio Valley in 1754. He was told to take the "Lands on the Ohio and waters thereof," and to widen the existing pack horse trail in order to accommodate wagons.

While at Will's Creek (present day Cumberland, Maryland), Washington learned that the French had taken Fort Prince George at the forks of the three rivers. He continued forward constructing the wagon trail across the Appalachian Mountains so that the British could have a route in order to retake the important location at the forks. He stopped fifty miles later in the Great Meadows, southeast of the forks, and set up camp.

While camped at Great Meadows, Washington received a message from Tanaghrisson, who was a Seneca governing for the Iroquois Confederacy in the Ohio River valley. Tanaghrisson held the title of Half King, and was an ally of the British. His message to Washington was that a band of French soldiers were nearby, and that they would attack Washington's camp. Washington took 40 of his soldiers through the dark, wet night of May 27, 1754 to the camp of Tanaghrisson, where warriors joined the party advancing on the French camp in a planned preemptive strike. As morning broke, they surprised the French camp under the command of Ensign Joseph Coulon de Villers de Jumonville. A skirmish that lasted only 15 minutes, with a number of shots fired, casualties and French captives, resulted in the French surrendering quickly. The Half King, not satisfied with the quick victory, killed the injured Jumonville with his tomahawk. The Half King was making a point that he wanted the French to leave the Ohio valley. These were the first shots of the yet undeclared French and Indian War. The skirmish was recalled by British historians as "The volley fired by a young Virginian in the backwoods of America set the world on fire."

The colonial forces returned to the Great Meadows camp and constructed a fort, aptly named, Fort Necessity. Washington's success was short-lived, for on July 3$^{rd}$, the French sent a large force from Fort Duquesne to attack Washington at Fort Necessity. After a day-long battle, the superior French forces took control of the battle and Washington was forced to surrender. In the terms of surrender, the French commander leniently allowed Washington and his troops to return to Virginia. The French and Indian War was now officially ongoing, and the French controlled all of the land west of the Allegheny Mountains.

In early 1755, the British, disturbed by the fact that the French controlled the confluence of the three rivers, sent General Edward Braddock to America as commander-in-chief of their forces in America. Braddock's primary intent was to take and control the most strategic and sought after location on the continent, namely the "Point" at the confluence of the Allegheny, Monongahela and Ohio Rivers. This meant that he had to take the French Fort Duquesne, which sat at the site.

Braddock, sixty years-old, would begin his quest by leading his troops from Virginia in June of 1755. He was to follow a plan set out by The Duke of Cumberland where he would cross the mountains with a 3,500-man army, and attack Fort Duquesne. Fort Duquesne was a symbol of French *hauteur*, and thus, it had to be taken and replaced by a British fort at the juncture of the gateway to the new world.

Braddock sailed on a convoy of twenty ships to America, and proceeded to Alexandria, Virginia for a meeting with their colonial allies. The Colonials argued against an attack on Fort Duquesne, and lobbied for an easier victory against the French at Fort Niagara in New York. This, they argued, would cut-off the French supply and their lifeline to the west. Braddock would hear none of the Colonial arguments. He had strict orders and that was to take the crown glory of New France, namely, Fort Duquesne. Once Fort Duquesne was taken, he would head north and move onto lesser quarry.

Braddock knew that he would need the colonies to take a great share of the load if he were to capture Fort Duquesne. He added their young, military-veteran, George Washington, as his aide, and headed for Fort Cumberland in Maryland. Here, supplies were found to be short, the Indian allies deserted, and quarrelling ensued between the British and the colonials.

The lone highlight of the month spent at the fort was the arrival of 150 wagons and 500 horses, sent by Benjamin Franklin of the Pennsylvania colony. Braddock made a point of taking a verbal shot at the other colonies by commenting that Pennsylvania had promised nothing and performed everything, while the other colonies promised everything and provided nothing.

Finally, six weeks behind schedule, the army received its marching orders on June 9, 1755. A 2,200-man army, with artillery and cavalry units, left Fort Cumberland in what some have said to be the most potent military force America had ever seen. The force consisted primarily of the British Forty-forth and Forty-Eighth Regiments, which included American recruits and various independent units from the American colonies. Only eight Indians remained and they were used as advance scouts.

As the army fought its way through the Allegheny Mountains, clearing a wider path as they moved, they were hampered by the weight of the artillery, and by a dwindling food supply. There were also rumors that the French were sending reinforcements to Fort Duquesne, and the need to reach the fort hastened. George Washington suggested that a column of 1,300 men be sent ahead to clear the path without the burden of carrying artillery and wagons. This turned out to be successful, and the army moved quickly behind the quickly clearing path.

On July 9th, they reached the Monongahela River, which was only a short distance from Fort Duquesne. The troops celebrated as their quarry was within sight. Washington fell ill during the latter part of the journey, but insisted on continuing on with the troops as they captured the "highest object of their wishes."

Fort Duquesne was known to consist of 600 French troops and 800 Indians, namely Shawnee, Delaware, Iroquois, and several others representing tribes from the Great Lakes. They were under the command of Captain Claude Pierre Pecaudy who understood Fort Duquesne would not stand up to an all-out attack with the inclusion of artillery. The French dispatched Captain Daniel-Marie Lienard de Beaujeu to the fort to take command, and he insisted on meeting the British while they were still in the forest. The Indians initially refused, but the captain worked hard to convince them to participate.

On the morning of July 9th, 250 French soldiers and 600 Native Americans moved quickly eastward in order to attempt to thwart the British advance. Setting up for an ambush, via the use of heavy forestation on a hillside, they waited for the army to come their way, but were initially surprised by the quick appearance of the British.

Both sides were surprised by the meeting, the French due to the timing, and the British due to the mere fact that the French were there. Obviously, the British scouts never saw the advancing French and Indian forces or did not have time to report. Each side quickly attempted to regroup, but the British had let their guard down since they did not anticipate any hostilities until they reached the outskirts of the fort. They were termed to be "panic stricken."

The British began to fire wildly, and their first shots were effective. French commander, Captain de Beaujeu, was immediately killed in the first volley. The French quickly regrouped under the command of Captain Jean Daniel Dumas, and he used the camouflage and hillside to strategically place his men in almost phantom positions.

The British, firing blindly into the forest, out of formation, and frightened by the lack of a visual enemy, abandoned their positions and "broke and ran as sheep before hounds." Their own artillery was left behind and used against them as they retreated. In two hours of fighting, the army lost one-thousand men, and sixty officers were hit while trying to restore order in the ranks.

General Braddock is said to have had four horses shot from under him, but continued until he was hit with an eventually fatal shot to the lungs. He was carried from the battlefield, and eventually passed away and was buried near Fort Necessity. George Washington, on horseback during the entire battle, left unscathed.

The command of the retreated British army, now in the vicinity of the abandoned Fort Necessity, was now in the hands of Colonel Thomas Dunbar. He still commanded an army of over a thousand men who could regroup, and make another advance on Fort Duquesne. He viewed the terror still on the faces of the men, and decided to march the entire force east to Philadelphia where, though only July, they intended to spend the winter.

This retreat did not sit well with the leaders of the American colonies, who so desperately wanted to have control of western Pennsylvania. Lieutenant Governor Dinwiddie of Virginia stated that Colonel Dunbar "appears to have determined to leave our frontiers as defenseless as possible." George Washington feared what "the consequences of the defeat would have upon our back (country) settlers."

The French did not gloat over the defeat of Braddock's powerful force. They were well aware of the consequences had they not totally caught the British and colonial forces by surprise. Their Native allies did take advantage of the victory and used it as a spring board to wreak havoc and terror throughout western Pennsylvania in 1755. The native warfare tactic of *petite guerre,* featured small numbers of swiftly moving groups who would strike settlements at dawn. They burned houses, and killed and scalped many of the settlers. At times, they would drag the settlers away in order to assimilate them into their dwindling tribes.

With the British army slumbering in Philadelphia, only George Washington's Virginia Regiment made attempts at scouring the forests for the roving bands. During 1756, Pennsylvania ordered the construction of a line of small forts in western Pennsylvania in order to protect the settlers. This proved to be ineffective, and the raiding continued until Pennsylvania Colonel John Armstrong retaliated by attacking the Delaware Indian stronghold at Kittanning. Armstrong led 300 Pennsylvanians in the attack, which surprised the Delaware, resulting in the death of their war chief.

The retaliation by the Pennsylvanians quelled the attacks only to a certain extent. Soon, the attacks again increased and this caused a major dilemma for the Quaker-controlled Pennsylvania. The Quakers believed in an orderly society, and peaceful relations with the Indians. They were hard-pressed to authorize continued attacks against the natives, in particular since the attacks were in western Pennsylvania, and not necessarily affecting Philadelphia. The Virginians gave their neighbors some advice..." The gentlemen of your country will either change their principals, or have their throat cut."

In 1758, under continued pressure, Pennsylvania continued with the construction of a chain of small forts in the western frontier. 1758 was also a year when the British decided to ignite their return to capture the hallowed ground at the forks of the Allegheny, Monongahela and Ohio Rivers. They were tired of four years of defeat in this quest and at the loss of lives and expense, which had resulted in nothing. At this time, William Pitt had come into power in Great Britain as Secretary of State. The tenacious Pitt took it upon himself to mold a plan that would capture Fort Duquesne, and give Britain the gateway to the west.

He created a plan that would attack New France in three different locations. While attacks would be on-going in two other locations, namely against French forts on the St. Lawrence River and Lake Champlain, the third army would find its way to attack Fort Duquesne, which could not rely of reinforcements due to the other engagements.

Part of William Pitt's plan was to assign the best and most energetic in the British service to see it through. As for his most desired campaign, the one against Fort Duquesne, he would choose Scottish Brigadier General John Forbes to plan the final phases and lead the attack. Pitt gave him young Colonel Henry Bouquet, a former member of the Swiss guards, to execute the campaign at the front. In addition, Colonel George Washington of the Virginia Regiment would lead the Americans.

In the spring of 1758, Forbes outlined his plans to take Fort Duquesne while in Philadelphia. His army would entail forty Royal Artillerists and would include the likes of the First Highland Battalion, the battalions of the Pennsylvania Regiment, several companies of the Royal American Regiment, two Virginia regiments, and detachments from Maryland, Delaware and North Carolina. The force was accompanied by Cherokee and Catawba warriors. This would be a combined army of 5,000 men.

With his army in place, General Forbes decided to follow the European strategy of Lancelot or a "Protected Advance." The army would move at a structured pace and, as it moved forward, it would build posts and supply bases at given intervals. He also decided to avoid the road already constructed by his predecessor, General Braddock, and follow the Raystown Indian Path over the rugged mountains and terrain in order to reach the forks at the three rivers. Their path would be called the "Forbes Road" and, by taking it, they would shorten their journey by 40 miles.

Colonel George Washington, knowing of the Virginia colony's interest in creating a commercial highway to the forks after the war, did not agree with the route that Forbes had chosen. He emphatically stated that "the beaten path (Braddock's) is the best passage through the mountains." Washington was very upset that the army continued to set out along the Raystown Indian Path and fumed "All is lost! All is lost, by heavens! Our enterprise will be ruined." "Forbes Road", would not benefit Virginia, as would that constructed by General Braddock, which originated from the south. They were correct in that assumption for "Forbes' Road" eventually became the first interstate highway in the United States, known as the Pennsylvania Turnpike.

By July of 1758, 1,200 men were advanced to cut the road through the Allegheny Mountain, which was deemed almost impenetrable. Under the command of Quartermaster Sir John St. Clair, they then continued to Laurel Hill or "Terrible Mountain," and then to Chestnut Ridge. The immense task resulted in a message sent by St. Clair stating, "The work to be done on this road is immense...send me as many men as you can with digging tools, this is a most diabolical work, and whiskey must be had."

By September 1$^{st}$, the army had advanced, though the Indians had abandoned them, and General Forbes ordered Pennsylvania Colonel James Burd, and Captain and engineer Harry Gordon, to construct a fort only fifty miles from Fort Duquesne. The fort, later to be named after General Ligonier, and called Fort Ligonier, would become the base for the bulk of the approaching army.

On September 9$^{th}$, Colonel Bouquet, at Fort Ligonier previous to General Forbes, determined that a reconnaissance mission to Fort Duquesne was in order. He permitted Major James Grant of the First Highland Regiment to lead 850 men to Fort Duquesne in order to assess French strength, and to finalize the plan of attack. This was a decision that completely went against the plan of General Forbes, who preferred a less risky approach to the impending battle.

On September 14$^{th}$, Major Grant's force sat atop a hill above Fort Duquesne. Before they realized it, they were surrounded by 800 French and Indians. A battle ensued and the British force suffered 300 casualties and the capture of Major Grant. The remainder to the force escaped and fell back to Fort Ligonier. General Forbes, learning of the unsuccessful mission, reprimanded Bouquet for possibly ruining the entire plan. The British had lost yet another battle over Fort Duquesne. General Forbes used the instance as an example of why his "Protected Advance" was the best course of action.

The French at Fort Duquesne, now under the command of Francois-Marie le Merchand, never celebrated their latest victory. They were well aware of the enormity of the fast-advancing British army, and they had also observed the lack of reinforcements and supplies, which were kept and/or stalled in order to defend on-going British attacks on French forts as far north as Canada.

Fort Duquesne was short of food, supplies and trade goods. The plan of Prime Minister William Pitt was working to perfection. Fort Duquesne, the crown jewel of the French holdings in New France, was now isolated, and must stand on its own. Their allied Indians from the Great Lakes, on the other hand, felt that the latest battle with the British had staved off an attack for another year and left the fort. This left only the Ohio warriors at the fort.

Francois-Marie le Marchand was wary that the British would learn of their dwindling defenses and weaknesses. He hoped that the British would winter at Fort Ligonier so that Fort Duquesne could be reinforced with men and supplies. Since he could not be certain that the British would wait until spring, he decided to make an offensive attack against them in order to delay their advance until that time.

On October 12, 1758, Captain Charles Phillippe Aubry led a force of 440 French troops and 150 Indians towards Fort Ligonier. Fort Ligonier was without Colonel Bouquet at the time, and command fell to Colonel Burd of the Pennsylvania Regiment. The French attacked the fort on that day, and were only held back by artillery of howitzers and mortars. The British and American forces that met the French were not successful in creating their retreat. Eventually, the French withdrew and returned to Fort Duquesne, but not before driving off most of Fort Ligonier's horses, and inflicting minor casualties. General Forbes and Colonel Bouquet were very upset that their much larger force did not completely defeat the French at such an opportunity.

While General Forbes, still on his way to Fort Ligonier, debated his next move, the Quakers once again attempted diplomatic measures to resolve the issue from across the state. Quaker Israel Pemberton, Jr., was the head of the Friendly Association for Regaining and Preserving Peace with the Indians by Pacific Measures, and his goal was to convince the Indian tribes not to support the French. This policy was endorsed by General Forbes, and by Pennsylvania Governor William Denny, who saw the Indians departure from the conflict as a means to end the war.

A Moravian missionary, by the name of Christian Frederic, carried forth official messages and gifts to the western Pennsylvania Indian nations. The messages conveyed peace and friendship, and the initial reaction was surprisingly very receptive. Frederic, by visiting the Indian nations, also provided Forbes with intelligence on the size and strength of the tribes in the area.

In October 1758, the work contributed by Israel Pemberton, Jr. and Christian Frederic resulted in thirteen Indian nations being represented at a meeting in Easton, Pennsylvania with the Governors of Pennsylvania and New Jersey, which was mediated by the Friendly Association. The result of the meeting was the Treaty of Easton, an implausible agreement by the Ohio Indians to permanently detach themselves from French forces.

Finally, with this new information in hand, General John Forbes reached Fort Ligonier (Loyalhanna) on November 2nd. The council of war met to determine the course of action, and determined that no further action would be taken against Fort Duquesne in 1758. They considered the fact that winter was approaching, and fifty miles of road were still needed to be built in order to reach the fort. The army would wait until spring.

On November 12th, a couple of incidents forced the council decision to be reversed. Colonel George Washington had recently arrived and soon had to lead his Virginia troops to reinforce another troop, which had been surprisingly attacked. During the melee, the Virginia troops ended up firing upon each other, forcing Washington to make his famous ride between the crossfire, pushing aside muskets with his sword and shouting for a ceasefire.

The battle resulted in vital information being provided by a British deserter, who was amongst the enemy. He readily provided information that the French were in dire straits at Fort Duquesne due to the lack of supplies and reinforcements. Forbes decided to move on Fort Duquesne before the two areas could be rectified, and sent a 2,500-man force and artillery on its way toward the Forks.

On November 24th, the army reached Turtle Creek, which was very near the field where General Braddock was defeated in the British's first quest for the fort. While camped there, they heard a great explosion and their forward scouts returned with news that Fort Duquesne was on fire. Immediately, a troop of horsemen were sent to investigate the situation.

The next day, the army reached a hillside overlooking the fort, and they could plainly see that nothing remained of it except for charred remains. It was apparent that the French, hearing of the advancing British army, blew up the fort and left the vicinity. Forbes gazed over the "Beautiful River" and relished in the fact that, finally, the hallowed ground was now British.

General Forbes' stay at the forks was no more than a week. He encouraged a day of celebration for his men, and renamed the vicinity around Fort Duquesne...Pittsburgh, in honor of the master of the entire expedition, Secretary of State William Pitt.

Shortly thereafter, Forbes made the long forty-three-day journey back to Philadelphia. Colonel George Washington, now that the ultimate victory had been accomplished, resigned from his commission and returned to civilian life. Without accommodations at the forks, and winter approaching, a great majority of the army fell back to Fort Ligonier. Colonel Hugh Mercer of the Continental army, close friend of George Washington, and veteran of the General Braddock and General Armstrong incursions into western Pennsylvania, was left to command two-hundred men, mostly Virginians, at the former site of Fort Duquesne. He was ordered to hold the site until a permanent British fortress could be built. Colonel Mercer worked hastily with his men in order to construct a temporary fort, which was named "Mercer's Fort."

Mercer was given the daunting task of holding the ground until spring. He was well aware of a possible French counter-attack, especially if they became aware of his limited defense capabilities. Mercer and his troops made it through the winter. In the early spring of 1759, the French gathered an army of 700 men, artillery, and 800 warriors, and planned to attack both Fort Ligonier and Pittsburgh's Mercer's Fort. They were only a day's travel from either when the attempt was thwarted. The French learned that Fort Niagara was under attack by the British and redirected the army to the greatest, current need.

William Pitt immediately ordered that Fort Pitt be built at the forks in Pittsburgh. Fort Pitt would, by far, be the largest, most extensive and elaborate fort in North America. Pitt's goal was to "Maintain his Majesty's subjects in undisputed possession of the Ohio." He sent more than one-hundred carpenters, bricklayers and brick makers, blacksmiths, masons, and the like to the site for the fort's construction, under the command of Captain Harry Gordon, the same man who built Fort Ligonier.

The constructed Fort Pitt was so large that the once formidable Fort Duquesne could stand solely within its parade ground. The fort encompassed eighteen acres of ground and had five sides in order to protect every flank. Fort Pitt, with its thick walls of brick and mud and enormous size, was constructed to be so formidable that the French would never again consider threatening Pittsburgh, and its vitally strategic location. The British now controlled the 'Gateway to the West', and they finally had their *Gibraltar* in America.

Fort Pitt was the primary catalyst that leads to the end of the French and Indian War and stood as a juggernaut through the Revolutionary War. It created the City of Pittsburgh and, due to its strategic location, was pronounced then and still today, as the "Gateway to the West."

Around 1760 and soon after the construction of Fort Pitt, a settlement of several hundred people began to develop around the fort. The settlement consisted primarily of early European settlers and traders, who are said to have built both cabins and houses in what they called "Uppertown and Lowertown."

At this time, Fort Pitt is still physically located in the Virginia colony. In the late 1750s and early 1760s, the Virginians, many of whom were part of the Colonial Army constructing the forts in Pittsburgh, began to move westward into the Ohio River valley. One of these soldiers, Robert Vance, constructed the first westward structure, a blockhouse fortification near the Ohio River, ten miles west of Fort Pitt in what is now the Borough of Coraopolis, Pennsylvania. This blockhouse (later surrounded by a stockade), known as Fort Vance, created the protection needed for the establishment of the first American westward settlement – which was the entire purpose of the French and Indian War. The war was fought over the control of the Point in Pittsburgh as a base for westward American expansion. The name Coraopolis is a Greek term for "Maiden City" or "First City," which establishes its historical significance. This is where the west began.

In 1763, Pontiac's Rebellion began, which was an attempt by Native Americans to drive out the British from western Pennsylvania. The Natives assaulted British forts in the Ohio Valley and their primary target would soon be Fort Pitt. Captain Simeon Ecuyer, a Swiss officer in command of Fort Pitt, heard of the pending attack and prepared accordingly. He stocked the fort with supplies and ordered all settlers into the fort. Pontiac's forces attacked the fort on June 22, 1763 and continued their siege for two months. The British dispatched Colonel Bouquet and several hundred soldiers to Pittsburgh to confront the Natives. Pontiac's warriors heard of Bouquet's advancing army and decided to attack them before they reached the fort. Bouquet's forces defeated Pontiac's warriors in the famous battle of Bushy Run. The siege of Fort Pitt ended after the victory and the British now had full control of the entire Ohio River Valley. In 1764, Colonel Bouquet constructed the Fort Pitt Blockhouse, which is the only remaining structure from Fort Pitt still standing today and the oldest authenticated building west of the Allegheny Mountains.

In 1768, the Iroquois signed the Fort Stanwix Treaty, which turned over land south of the Ohio River to the British. With this treaty in place, Colonial and European expansion into the Ohio valley increased. It is estimated that between 4,000 to 5,000 families settled in western Pennsylvania during the period of 1768 and 1770. Most of these settlers were either English or Scotch-Irish, but the Welsh and Germans were also known to have been in the area. Because of the fear of raids by Native Americans, the settlers often built their cabins near water sources and they also constructed central blockhouses, where neighbors would gather during conflicts. Overall, these groups created what may be deemed as farming communities. The British army left Fort Pitt in 1772 and it was left to the colonists for their own protection.

In 1773, Governor Lord Dunmore decided to reassert Virginia's claim to Pittsburgh. He claimed Fort Pitt and renamed it Fort Dunmore. Because of this action, the colonies of Virginia and Pennsylvania waged a long civil and, at times, physical battle over the rights to Western Pennsylvania and Pittsburgh in 1773 and 1774. Pennsylvania eventually was granted the land, but this wasn't until the late 1770's and into the early 1780's.

**American Revolution**

In 1774, during the Pennsylvania-Virginia battle over Pittsburgh, what is known as Dunmore's War also began, which was a result of attacks in the Ohio River valley by the Wyandot, Miami and Shawnee tribes, who were defending their hunting grounds from further colonial settlements. The colonists were victorious in the conflict, but skirmishes continued throughout the American Revolution. The Native Americans hoped that the Revolutionary War would lead to the expulsion of the American colonists from their lands, if the British were victorious.

Though Pittsburgh played a major role in the French & Indian War, it played a significantly lesser role in the Revolutionary War. In 1777, during the now on-going American Revolution, the Continental Army reestablishes Fort Pitt as its western headquarters and it was placed under the command of General Edward Hand. Fort Pitt housed troops and supplies for the new United States. There are no Revolutionary War conflicts known to have taken place in Pittsburgh.

In 1778, the first peace treaty between the United States and Native Americans – the Delaware Indians - was signed at Fort Pitt. This was known as the Treaty of Fort Pitt or the Delaware Treaty. The only military expedition from the fort during the war period was in 1779 when Colonel Daniel Brodhead led 600 men from Fort Pitt to destroy Seneca villages along the upper Allegheny. In the 1784, in the Treaty of Fort Stanwix, the Iroquois ceded the land north of the Purchase Line to Pennsylvania.

**Post Revolution and the Lewis & Clark Expedition**

After the Revolution, the village of Pittsburgh began to prosper and industries were established. The area was known for its boat building, in particular flatboats, which were used by settlers and pioneers to move goods downriver. By 1792, the boatyards had constructed one of the first sloop boats, called the *Western Experiment*. The boat building industry became a larger component of the Pittsburgh economy. The yards began to produce larger boats and by the turn of the 19th century they were building ocean-going vessels that could deliver goods as far as Europe. In 1811, the first steamboat was built in Pittsburgh.

Another local industry that prospered was that of rye whiskey. Whiskey was used as a form of currency in frontier times and there was no better place to make it than the Gateway to the West. Shortly thereafter the manufacturing of glass began, driven by the need to bottle the whiskey. To show how quickly culture became established in Pittsburgh, in 1787, the University of Western Pennsylvania was created, which became the University of Pittsburgh in 1908.

Fort LaFayette was built in 1791 after Fort Pitt was abandoned and the residents demanded military protection against Indian attacks. Fort LaFayette was constructed with a stockade and four bastions and was located in what is now the Downtown section of the city. Fort Layfayette stood until 1815.

In 1794, the federal government imposed an excise tax on whiskey. Western Pennsylvania farmers felt victimized, since they were a primary source of the product. The farmers rebelled and marched on Pittsburgh, which is now known as the Whiskey Rebellion. President George Washington quelled the rebellion quickly by sending in militias from several states.

Pittsburgh's reputation as a center for boat building was emphasized by the Lewis and Clark Expedition. Lewis spent six-weeks in Pittsburgh waiting for the construction of the expedition's 55-foot keelboat. Once complete, Lewis commissioned eleven locals for the expedition, as well as a dog and supplies, and began the journey on Pittsburgh's rivers to meet up with Clark. The Lewis and Clark expedition is formally stated as beginning in Pittsburgh for this reason.

## War of 1812

Commerce, such as general stores, bakeries and various shops, continued to be an essential part of Pittsburgh's early economy, but manufacturing grew steadily. The Pittsburgh region was abundant with many natural resources, such as coal, lumber, natural gas, oil and farmland.

The War of 1812 with Britain established Pittsburgh as a manufacturing capital. Britain had historically supplied most of the manufactured goods for the United States, but with the on-going war with Britain the goods ceased to arrive. In addition, the British blockade of the American coast increased the need for American-made goods and the U.S. turned to Pittsburgh. The city produced the needed brass, tin, glass and iron and became the country's manufacturing hub.

In 1814, the government decommissioned Fort Lafayette and constructed the Allegheny or Pittsburgh Federal Arsenal on Pittsburgh's North Side, which stood until 1909. The Arsenal would be used as the nation's primary source for constructing defense weapons.

In the coming decades, many improvements were made to the transportation infrastructure. In 1818, the region's first river bridge, the Smithfield Street Bridge, opened. This bridge was the first of many in what would make the city the "City of Bridges." In 1834, the Pennsylvania Main Line Canal was completed, making Pittsburgh part of a transportation system that included rivers, roads, and canals. In 1835, the first locomotive west of the Alleghenies was built in Pittsburgh.

By the 1840s, Pittsburgh was already one of the largest cities west of the Appalachian Mountains. In 1840, the original Pennsylvania Turnpike was completed, connecting Pittsburgh and Philadelphia. By 1851, the railroads became a major means of transportation and the lines were certain to connect to the city. The Ohio and Pennsylvania Railroad began service between Cleveland and Pittsburgh and, in 1854, the Pennsylvania Railroad began service between Pittsburgh and Philadelphia. In 1859, coke-fire smelting also became prominent in the region. Through the advent of the railroads and its manufacturing base, Pittsburgh had grown into an industrial powerhouse.

### The Civil War

Pittsburgh was, once again, spared the savages of war during the internal American conflict, though the city did play a major role for the Union as the primary source of armaments. At the Pittsburgh Federal Arsenal, the city constructed iron-clad warships, cannons and the world's first 21-inch gun. The Pittsburgh Federal Arsenal, also known as the Allegheny Arsenal, as well as the Fort Pitt Foundry, were major suppliers of iron and munitions for the Union Army during the Civil War. The city also maintained an extensive transportation system enabling military equipment to be moved by rail, ground or water. With the need for these military goods the Civil War boosted the city's economy. Nationwide, Pittsburgh was called the "Arsenal of the Union."

The Confederate Army realized the importance of Pittsburgh to the Union Army and set its sights on attacking the city. As the Confederate Army marched towards the famous battle of Gettysburg (Pennsylvania), two attempts were made by other Confederate units to distract the Union Army away from Gettysburg. One was known as Morgan's Raid, under the command of Brig. General John Hunt Morgan, which was an incursion of Confederate cavalry units moving into Indiana and Ohio during June 1863. The other movement was the Jones-Imboden Raid, which sent Confederate units into what is now West Virginia. In both circumstances, Pittsburgh was an ultimate target and the troops were within a day of reaching the city, but the Union Army thwarted both incursions before any attempt could be made.

History states that the Confederate Army planned to march on Pittsburgh as soon as it was victorious at Gettysburg. The U.S. War Department was very concerned of the possibility, based on intercepted intelligence, and established a formal Federal military presence in Pittsburgh. The Army dispatched General William T.H. Brooks to organize the defense of the city. Brooks authorized the construction of a series of small forts on the eastern outskirts of the city. Local citizens were asked to assist in the construction, which they did. Four forts were constructed – Fort Robert Smalls, Fort Laughlin, Fort Jones and Fort Black. It is also stated that 23 other smaller redoubts were constructed. Fort Black was the largest of the forts and would be the primary post to defend the city.

Some of these forts were still under construction when the battle at Gettysburg occurred. Once the Union was victorious at Gettysburg and the Confederates retreated, the city was deemed to be no longer in danger.

## Post-Civil War

Beginning in the 1870s, the economy shifted from smaller manufacturers to mass production facilities. Production of steel began in 1875, creating modern plants and integrated mills, which was emphasized by the first steel rail be manufactured. The economy increased resulting in the rapid growth of steel, glass, coke and railroad goods. Pittsburgh provided the needed steel and products for the United State war efforts in the Spanish-American War. By 1911, Pittsburgh was producing half of the nation's steel and one-third of the glass production.

Some of the greatest names in American history built their companies and their fortunes in Pittsburgh. Industrialists such as Charles Schwab, George Westinghouse, Andrew Carnegie, Henry Clay Frick and Andrew W. Mellon created an industrial empire. From these individuals and families came great American companies, such as U.S. Steel, ALCOA, Westinghouse, Charles Schwab and Mellon Bank (now Bank of New York-Mellon), as well as Carnegie Hall, the Carnegie Museum system and the Carnegie Library system.

## World War I

Pittsburgh's manufacturing base was pivotal to the American military during World War I. The city constructed most the Allies' armaments, thus being designated as the *Arsenal of the Allies*. The city was also key to the manufacturing of optical glass, used in binoculars, telescopes and rifles, as well as developing the world's first gas mask. Pittsburgh also sent 60,000 men and women to support the American effort in World War I.

## World War II

As in World War I, Pittsburgh produced the munitions for the Allied war effort in World War II. Pittsburgh actually produced more military-related equipment than all of the Allied countries combined. The city that had been called the Arsenal of the Union in the Civil War, the Arsenal of the Allies in World War I, was now being designated as the "Arsenal of Democracy."

The Pittsburgh area also developed the Jeep and the new class of attack landing crafts used during the Allied invasion of Normandy and in the Pacific. Pittsburgh also created the *We Can Do It!* – Rosie the Riverter – rallying cry campaign. Of course, the Tuskegee Airmen hailed from Pittsburgh and thousands of locals were sent to support the war effort.

The steel industry continued to make the required steel and armaments necessary for the United States war efforts in the **Korean** and **Vietnam Wars**.

## Post World War II

Following World War II, as the industrial base continued to grow; Pittsburgh determined a need to control the effects of industry and launched a very successful clean air movement. In addition, it created one of the country's most successful civic revitalization projects known as the "Renaissance." During the Renaissance period, Pittsburgh transformed its Downtown with parks, plazas and new skyscrapers.

In the 1970's, foreign competition led to the collapse of the steel industry. Eventually, this resulted in mill closures and massive layoffs, leading to the demise of a majority of the steel industry and several other industries dependent upon it. The area was too dependent on manufacturing and many jobs were lost, forcing many to move elsewhere to find employment. It is said that western Pennsylvania lost an entire generation during the 1970's and 1980's.

Many of these displaced residents living throughout the country still call Pittsburgh home.

At the turn of the century, Pittsburgh's population stagnated, but the tide was positively turning. The population of the Pittsburgh metropolitan area held steady and began to show small increases. This influx is related to one of the greatest turnarounds in history, as Pittsburgh transformed itself from a manufacturing economy into an economy based on high technology, education, medicine and corporate headquarters. Robotics, software creation, engineering, medical research, educational research, Fortune 500 companies and small business, combined with a smaller manufacturing footprint, has created a model that is studied by cities throughout the world. It has attracted significant investments from Google, Facebook, Uber, Microsoft, Disney, Apple, Amazon, Intel and Netflix – some of the best companies in the country. This new Renaissance has attracted talent from across the world, as well as the return of Pittsburghers who were forced to leave in the 1980's. In addition, the city that was once a bastion for European immigrants is finally realizing immigration gains from Asia, India and Latin America.

In present-day Pittsburgh, the diversified economy, a low cost of living and a rich infrastructure for education and culture has made its future very bright. It is often ranked as one of the "World's Most Livable Cities" and it is well-deserved. The city has recognized significant construction in Downtown condo and apartment complexes, making its Downtown the fastest growing neighborhood in the city. Tourism has recently boomed in Pittsburgh – it's been ranked as the top tourist destination in the State – and has realized over 3,000 new hotel rooms opening in the past decade. Occupancy rates at the hotels and Downtown office towers consistently have higher occupancy than in comparable cities. The region has also become a leader in green environmental design, emphasizing a complete transformation. It is currently the home of one of the largest "green" buildings in the world – The David L. Lawrence Convention Center and the first convention center to be LEED certified.

**Visiting Historic Sites**

The location of the forts at the Point in Pittsburgh can be visualized through a visit to beautiful Point State Park in Downtown Pittsburgh. Point State Park is the home of the Fort Pitt Museum, which provides some of the greatest detail and houses some of the best artifacts of the French and Indian War. The park also contains an original blockhouse of Fort Pitt, the oldest standing structure in the city, and designations of the actual location of the fort.

Fort LaFayette, located in Downtown, is designated by a historical marker and the Pittsburgh Federal Arsenal has relics of its existence located in Arsenal Park on the North Side. Visiting Pittsburgh and its place in American history would not be complete without a visit to Soldiers and Sailors Memorial Hall (located in the Oakland section next to the University of Pittsburgh). This hall maintains authentic military relics and memorabilia of most of the U.S. wars that took place. In addition, The Senator John Heinz Regional History Center (associated with Smithsonian Institution) located in the Strip District, has a collection of French and Indian War Memorabilia. The Pittsburgh area encompasses a great deal of French and Indian War sites that may be toured. The Bushy Run Battlefield (Jeannette, Pennsylvania), Fort Necessity (Farmington, Pennsylvania) and Fort Ligonier (Ligonier, Pennsylvania) are all within a short drive of Pittsburgh.

# Bibliography

VisitPittsburgh.com

TrustArts.org

Pittsburgh Downtown Partnership

Pittsburgh Post-Gazette

Pittsburgh Tribune-Review

Pittsburgh Film Office

Pittsburgh Magazine

Pittsburgh Quarterly

Pittsburgh Business Times

DowntownPittsburgh.com

Paris of Appalachia – Brian O'Neill – Carnegie Mellon University Press (2009)

Numerous websites, newspaper, magazine and online articles.

Wikipedia

History of Allegheny County, Pennsylvania
Samuel W. Durant
Philadelphia: L.H. Everts, 1876

History of Allegheny County, Pennsylvania
Chicago: A. Warner Co., 1889

Genealogical and Personal History of western Pennsylvania
Jordan, John W. (John Woolf)
New York: Lewis Historical Publishing Company, 1915

Pittsburgh in 1816
Pittsburgh: Carnegie Library, 1916

Frontier Retreat on the Upper Ohio
Louise Phelps Kellogg
Madison: The Society, 1917

Old and New Westmoreland
John Newton Boucher
New York: The American Historical Society, 1918

History of Pittsburgh
George Thornton Fleming
New York, Chicago: The American Historical Society, Inc., 1922

Where the West Began; A story of Coraopolis and the Ohio Valley
Edward B. Maurey
Coraopolis, PA: Record Publishing Company, 1930

Annals of southwestern Pennsylvania
Lewis Clark Walkinshaw
New York: Lewis Historical Publishing Company, Inc., 1939

The French and Indian War in Pennsylvania
Louis M. Waddell and Bruce D. Bomberger
Harrisburg, PA: Pennsylvania Historical and Museum Comm., 1996

Coraopolis Semi-Centennial Publication
Horace Thomas, Jr.
Coraopolis, PA: Coraopolis Chamber of Commerce, 1960

Old Fort Vance
Louise Woodbridge Dippold
Sewickley, PA: Sewickley Herald. 1911

War for Empire in Western Pennsylvania
J. Martin West
Pittsburgh: Fort Ligonier Association, 1993

Revolutionary War Timeline
Thehistoryplace.com

University of Pittsburgh Digital Library
Pittsburgh: 2007

The Library of Virginia
Richmond, VA: 2007

Coraopolis Centennial Publication
Coraopolis, PA: Wadsworth Publishing, 1986

Coraopolis – Pictures

Fort Pitt Museum, Pittsburgh
Historical Society of western Pennsylvania
Pennsylvania Historical and Museum Commission
Coraopolis Historical Society
Historical Society of Sewickley Valley
Coraopolis Memorial Library
Sewickley Library
Senator John Heinz Pittsburgh Regional History Center

# About the Author

Rock DiLisio is from Pittsburgh, Pennsylvania and is also the author of - Italy Central - Abruzzo Travel Guide.  His family also once owned a travel agency near the Pittsburgh International Airport.  His other books include:  Night in the Galaxies, Archaeology In-Brief, American Advance, Alba's Abruzzo, Firings from the Fox Hole, Sherlock Holmes: Mysteries of the Victorian Era, Three Kings of Casablanca, Stone of the Sahara and Palace of the Pharaoh.

Printed in the United States
By Bookmasters